2013

NHL DRAFT GUIDE

I0220919

© 2013 by The Hockey Press

All rights reserved.

ISBN-13: 978-0991677535
ISBN-10: 0991677536

HP Story

In 2004 I was coaching Wayne Simmonds in AAA hockey. It was crystal clear to me that Wayne had elite talent. I wondered how a player so talented could go under the radar and be completely missed by the hockey world for so long. It was midway through that season that I had the idea, and HockeyProspect.com was born.

This has been HockeyProspect.com's best year to date. We added more great team members and once again, we saw more games in more places than ever before.

I'm proud of the people involved with HockeyProspect.com. They are huge fans of the game and are passionate about their crafts, whether it be scouting, writing or video work. We have some truly talented scouts and equally talented writers and interviewers. The summer of 2013 will be spent on refining our service and making improvements to make next season even better.

Mark Edwards
Founder & Director of Scouting
HockeyProspect.com

Acknowledgements

This book would not have been possible without the efforts and long hours put in by our team of both scouts and writers. All of our team members are dedicated and love the sport.

To all the photographers who show off their talents in the photos we use both in this draft guide and on our website. Thanks for making the game come to life through your photos.

We also want to thank Paul Krotz of the CHL and all the folks at the NHL, OHL,WHL, QMJHL, IIHF, USHL, USA Hockey and of course Hockey Canada for their support and assistance.

Thanks,

Mark Edwards

Contents

1

SCOUTING REPORTS

Nathan Mackinnon

Center – Halifax Mooseheads
Born Sep 1 1995 – Cole Harbour, NS
Height 6.00 - Weight 182 - Shoots R

HOCKEYPROSPECT.COM

ROUND ONE #1

Games	Goals	Assists	Points	PIMS	+/-
44	32	43	75	45	+40

Nathan MacKinnon is an elite player. A tremendous skater, his first few strides are really what distinguishes him from other players, he can get to top speed with a few strides and get past a defenseman quickly. His top speed is superb and his lateral movements are just as good. He can turn on a dime, stop and start easily or twist and turn abruptly in a one-on-one confrontation to create space. He is blessed with amazing puck handling skills that he uses at top speed. Nathan is a great goal scorer and finds shooting lanes to get that strong and quick release wrist shot on net from just about anywhere. He excelled eluding defensive coverage; which is saying something, considering he was always paired against the opposing teams' best defensive duo. He has great passing skills, but is probably viewed as a goal scorer more than a playmaker.

MacKinnon has a great work ethic. He will get the dirty goals in traffic, he will take a hit to make a play or retrieve a lose puck. MacKinnon can simplify the skills and speed game to a chippy North-South game and be as effective. He's a versatile performer. Defensively, Nathan MacKinnon is dedicated and he has progressed nicely in his play without the puck since his first game in the QMJHL. His strength is great, which gives him solid balance on his skatesWhile not a menacing physical player, he can lay the body on occasion and he will engage a physical battle on the wall.

Mackinnon will sometimes put too much pressure on himself when things aren't going right. He will still work as hard as he can, but not wisely. He also could improve his game management, meaning the importance of choosing the right times to simplify his game. We think this will get better as he plays more defensive minutes. He was on such a stacked team in Halifax this year, he rarely had to do so.

MacKinnon's professional potential is huge. With the skill, speed and competitive nature he possesses he will become a highly dynamic point producer in the NHL. His work ethic and character should be huge factors for him when facing adversity. With more maturity there is no reason why Nathan MacKinnon won't live up to the hype. Regardless of who selects Nathan at the 2013 NHL Entry Draft, we expect him to make the jump to the NHL immediately.

Seth Jones

Defense - Portland Winterhawks
Born October 3 1994 – Frisco, TX
Height 6.03.5 - Weight 205 - Shoots R

Games	Goals	Assists	Points	PIMS	+/-
61	14	42	56	33	+46

It is rare to find a complete package in a defenseman like Seth Jones. He can make an impact at both ends of the ice in every game he plays with his size, athleticism, intelligence and hockey skills. He has caught the attention of the entire hockey world it seems with his play this year, and which ever team that is able to pick him up in the NHL Entry Draft this year will have their hands on a franchise defenseman for years to come.

One of the most impressive attributes of Seth Jones is his skating ability given his size. He is very mobile in all areas of the ice. He can make quick pivots and fast stops and starts along the walls to contain an opponent, quickly accelerate and reach top end speed to go coast to coast for a scoring chance or quickly skate backwards and maintain an excellent gap on the quickest players in the league. Offensively, Jones seems to have all the tools. He has very good vision and quarterbacks a lethal power play. He recognizes when he can push the play, and when to be patient and wait for his forwards to get into position. He makes excellent passes to get the attack going, but he does have the tendency to try to force plays at times. Jones also has a rocket of a shot from the point, and makes it miserable on opposing goaltenders, especially when there is a screen in front of them as Jones does a good job of getting shots on net. Jones has also been able to score a few coast to coast goals this year. He uses his speed, long reach and stick handling abilities to get around opponents and score some nice goals.

Jones is a force in his own zone. He maintains an excellent gap and uses his long reach. He is able to be aggressive because of his speed. He consistently uses his great stick to take away passing lanes and deflect away anything that comes to the slot. He is so strong along the boards, and is great at tying up opponents. He has the abilities to land big hits in the neutral zone and force opponents to be wary as they enter the neutral zone. The biggest concern for Jones is his lack of intensity in his play at times. He certainly shows up for big games, as evident by his performance in the World Juniors. He needs to be the best player on his team every night and will surely be counted on to be a leader on his team wherever he goes, but without the high level of intensity and interest in every game, it may be a concern in the future.

2

Jonathan Drouin

Left Wing – Halifax Mooseheads
Born March 27 1995 – Ste-Agathe, QC
Height 5.10.5 - Weight 186 - Shoots L

ROUND ONE #3

Games	Goals	Assists	Points	PIMS	+/-
49	41	64	105	32	+48

What an amazing season it was for Jonathan Drouin, from start to finish. He left a strong impression on us at our first viewing early in the year and he kept accumulating solid outings from that moment on.

Drouin's play with the puck is clearly special and he would seem to be a lock as a point producer at the NHL,level. His game is about elite speed, vision and puck handling abilities combined with perhaps the smartest player in the draf t. He has extremely quick feet and a very good explosiveness that allows him to transition from one zone to another in a hurry. Drouin is also extremely creative using his quick hands that creates the opportunity to elude extra defenders on his way to the offensive zone. As a puck carrier, he was not stopped often this season. Regardless of some risky plays he tries at times, he always manages to get the puck back on his stick and keep going.

Drouin excels when managing the puck in the offensive zone, where he is just as good shooting the puck as passing it. He showed off his laser wrist shot on numerous occasions this season, leaving the goalies little chance when he lets it go. It's a very quick and accurate shot that he rapidly fires. Drouin can also set up magnificent plays for his teammates with great vision and accuracy. He is a very natural player with the puck and the decisions he makes are always quick and in the flow of the game. His offensive instincts are extremely sharp, allowing him to play with great confidence. Defensively, Drouin was fairly dedicated and has made some good progress. It was not rare to see Drouin create a few turnovers in a game with his strong sense of anticipation.

Quotable: "One things that stood out for me in my early viewings of him was his ability to create time and space for himself. I saw him hold of defenders dogging him all over the offensive zone and he used his feet, creativity and puck handling skills to buy himself time until he could make a smart play. Drouin is up with my fave prospects I have ever scouted because he provides so much excitement. I'll remember a goal he scored in Drummondville for a long time. He could easily have been the first player taken in a draft without guys named Seth Jones and Nathan Mackinnon." - Mark Edwards

Valeri Nichushkin

Right Wing –Chelyabinsk (KHL)
Born March 4 1995 – Chelyabinsk, RUS
Height 6.04 - Weight 202 - Shoots L

Games	Goals	Assists	Points	PIMS	+/-
18	4	2	6	0	+6

Valeri is a forward who has impressed us over the last two years growing from a good prospect, to a great prospect. Every time we saw Valeri he seemed to be improving making the 2012-2013 season very intriguing for him. Valeri moved up the ranks from the MHL to Chelmet Chelyabinsk of the VHL and finally finishing his season and playing most of his games with Traktor Chelyabinsk of the KHL. Valeri continued his international representation of his country playing at the 2013 World Junior Championships and the 2013 IIHF U18 Championships.

Valeri has tremendous size and has an effective skating ability that can best be compared to Alex Galchenyuk's or Evgeni Malkin's skating style where all are big bodied and have a crouched down skating style. All three have deceptive speed to go with their size. Valeri protects the puck and will fearlessly drive the net. Despite his size he is surprisingly elusive and can utilize his hands and some moves to evade checkers and score some absolutely beautiful goals. His physical game has grown a bit over the last few years he's more willing to give and receive hits than he used to be and makes him much more effective. It's still not a big part of his game, but his comfort level is increasing. Valeri is more of a goal scorer and has a shot that is already better than the average NHL players shot and will allow him to score right away in the league. He prefers to shoot the puck way over passing it, which actually results in Valeri having a deceptive ability to pass the puck and create plays. We've watched moments where he simply didn't have a shooting lane, sometimes he will force it, but when he passes he completes some moderately difficult passes tape to tape. Valeri is intelligent with his positioning and makes himself an available shooting option for passers.

Nichushkin has shown us some flashes of competitiveness outside of the offensive zone forcing turnovers and being aggressive on the puck carrier. Valeri is one of the top prospects for the 2013 NHL Entry Draft. His willingness to come to North America to play certainly will alter the shape of this draft near the top and he has shown us clear signs of being able to contribute at the NHL level right away.

4

Aleksander Barkov

Center – Tappara (SM-liiga)
Born Sep 2 1995 – Tampere, Finland
Height 6.03 - Weight 205 – Shoots L

Games	Goals	Assists	Points	PIMS	+/-
53	21	27	48	8	+18

Aleksander has been on the radar for the 2013 NHL Entry Draft for a few years now. It's hard to believe if Barkov was born just two weeks later he would be ineligible until the 2014 NHL Entry Draft. In 2010-2011 a 15 year old Barkov really had his gian bridge in development rapidly rising through the U16 and U18 programs posting nearly a point per game in the U20 league. In 2011-2012 as a 16 year old Barkov posted 16 points in 32 games in Finland's top mens league showing his true potential, also participating in the 2012 World Junior Championships. Aleksander can't even be considered an adult in North America until September 2013, but he looked like a man amongst boys finishing in the top 10 scoring in Finland's top men's league this past season.

Barkov is a big strong forward who showed particularly in the World Junior Championships when matched up against players his own age that he is capable of asserting himself with his size. He is strong on the puck, protecting it effectively and can possess the puck for long periods of time. This is increasingly dangerous because of the high level of creativity Barkov possesses. He can produce points very well, but he does so using a great combination of shooting and passing ability. He is an unpredictable player because if you play his shot, he'll make a great pass, and if you play the pass he'll fire a hard, accurate shot on net. Barkov is capable of taking up space out front of the opposing net. Because of his size he is very difficult to move out front. This is something he's had to learn because he was a bit more on the perimeter. If you can move him from the front,

Barkov will find good positioning in the offensive zone. He is great along the boards and wins a lot of battles showing strength and relentlessness along the boards. He also forechecks hard creating turnovers. Barkov's skating ability needs to improve. It is expected at his size and age that it is something that needs work and will be the biggest area of focus during the summer to help Barkov be NHL ready come September. He shows good backcheck and competes hard defensively. He has also shown well in the face-off circle winning a lot of key draws for his teams.

Barkov is expected to be one of the first names called at the 2013 NHL Entry Draft. He shows a ton of upside as a forward who could walk onto an NHL roster immediately and help a team at the NHL level right away. He has a big upside and whichever team selects Aleksander will be very happy on June 30th.

Sean Monahan

Center – Ottawa 67's (OHL)
Born October 12 1994, Brampton, ONT
Height 6.02.25 - Weight 187 - Shoots L

Games	Goals	Assists	Points	PIMS	+/-
43	8	9	17	33	+3

Monahan was a bright spot on a team that did not have very much of that this season. He projects to be a top ten pick in the 2013 NHL Entry Draft and we believe he has the potential to be selected in the top five. He was drafted 16th overall by the Ottawa 67s at the 2010 OHL Priority Selection Draft out of the Mississauga Rebels Minor Midget program. He made the 67's in his 16 year old season and represented Ontario in the World U-17 Hockey Challenge. Sean went into his sophomore season looking to make an impact and with the departure of key players along with a few injuries, Monahan was launched into the spotlight and did an incredible job helping Ottawa capture the 2012 East Division Title. Due to his late birth date he was ineligible for the draft in his second season and needed to return to Ottawa where his 67's were in full rebuild mode.

Monahan has demonstrated the ability to take control of a game and become a factor in every offensive opportunity that takes place when he is on the ice. He possesses incredible patience with the puck that allows him to get to the slot with the puck and find time and space to work with. He has a very accurate shot that can beat goaltenders clean without traffic in front of the net off the rush which is one reason why he has scored 84 goals in his first 3 seasons in the OHL. It is also a tribute to his positioning as he can slip in and out of areas in the offensive zone undetected and always seems to be in the absolute idea positioning. He has solid speed to come off the wing then lets his deadly shot go and can pick his spots with ease. He has great hands and moves with the puck to create space and cycles the puck very effectively. The 67's coaching staff recognized his ability to play in all three zones and used him both on the power play and the penalty kill throughout the season. He gets his stick in lanes to deflect passes out of danger on the penalty kill

Monahan should become a top six forward at the NHL level who plays a complete game working hard in all three zones. He may need another year at the junior level to continue developing where he would be a critical part of Canada's 2014 World Junior Championship Roster. However it wouldn't be a surprise to see him get a 9 game tryout and see where it goes from there.

Elias Lindholm

Center – Brynas (SEL)
Born Dec 2 1994 – Boden, Sweden
Height 6.00 - Weight 192 Shoots R

Games	Goals	Assists	Points	PIMS	+/-
48	11	19	30	2	+1

Elias Lindholm first caught the attention of HockeyProspect.com during the 2011 World Jr. A Challenge Tournament. He was undoubtedly the best player, and has since been touted as the best player available in the 2013 NHL Entry Draft from Sweden by many scouts.

It is difficult to not notice Lindholm when he is out on the ice. He always seems to be around the puck and plays with such a high intensity at all times. He positions himself properly without the puck to give himself a chance to be a target for a pass or to make a great defensive play. Lindholm battles hard for loose pucks, and backchecks extremely hard. He makes smart stick checks from behind and is able to create takeaways after takeaways and get a quick transition play started for his team.

Offensively, Lindholm is a very skilled playmaker. He sees the ice extremely well, and seems to be very aware of everything around him. He is very patient and allows the play to develop before he makes a play with the puck, and he is able to do so because of his good stickhandling abilities and his quickness out in open ice. In terms of his passing ability, he can make tape to tape saucer passes in traffic if necessary, or quickly send a backhand pass to a teammate in the slot from behind the net through a few sticks. He really makes his linemates look better because he is able to find them anywhere out on the ice and give them a chance to score. One area of improvement for Lindholm with the puck would be his ability to finish off plays. He gets very good chances around the net, but just does not seem to be able to score on them as often as he should, and he should also try to look to shoot more often. He could get a little predictable and opponents may start to anticipate passes and intercept them more easily.

Defensively, Lindholm is a very polished player without the puck. Not only does he play with a lot of intensity, but he also possesses a high level of hockey sense. He seems to be able to pick off passes easily as he puts himself in good position, and anticipates the play quite well. He will block shots fearlessly, and displays his high level of competitiveness again and again during battles for loose pucks.

Nikita Zadorov

Defenseman – London Knights (OHL)
Born April 15 1995 – Moscow, Russia
Height 6.05.25 - Weight 221 - Shoots L

Games	Goals	Assists	Points	PIMS	+/-
63	6	19	25	54	+33

Nikita was selected 9th Overall in the 2012 CHL Import Draft by the London Knights. Nikita spent his 2011-2012 season with CSKA-Krasnaja Armija Moskva of the MHL in Russia. He first showed what he was capable of in North America at the 2012 World U17 Challenge. He had a fairly strong performance for Team Russia en route to helping them win Gold. He also participated in the IIHL World U18 Championships scoring twice as an under-ager at the tournament. He impressed the Knights who were willing to take him very high and bring him over to the OHL. The Knights placed him in the 3rd pairing to start the season and slowly increased his minutes as the season moved along.

The first things you notice about Nikita is his skating and his size. He is very good skater and we expect he will continue to improve as he gains strength. Nikita is also a very physical player who takes pride in finishing his hits. This was an area we saw tremendous improvements this season. Early in the season, he would chase hits and put himself out of position, making his team outnumbered down low. Now he regularly lets the play come to him, maintaining much better one on one positioning. He will still use his body effectively, but will pick his spots and do it at intelligent times. Nikita has underrated puck skills and is capable of skating the puck up ice and gaining the offensive zone. Another area he has improved is his puck handling ability. He was hit or miss early in the year but now he's a lot more consistent and intelligent with both his decisions and actual puck skills. He's effective holding the offensive line and generally can get his shot through from the point with smart shooting decisions. Nikita has shown the ability and intelligence to pinch in off the line during sustained pressure in the offensive zone which resulted in some scoring opportunities for Zadorov and his team. He is smart and generally won't attempt this unless there is little risk.

Nikita has provided some offense at the junior level while playing a solid defensive game making him a valuable defenseman at both ends. Right now, Nikita looks more like a physical shutdown defenseman who is just now discovering his offensive potential. His overall shooting ability needs improvement.

Rasmus Ristolainen

Defense – TPS (SM-liiga)
Born October 27 1994 – Turku, Finland
Height 6.04 - Weight 207 - Shoots R

Games	Goals	Assists	Points	PIMS	+/-
52	3	12	15	32	-7

Ristolainen is an aggressive offensive defenseman who always looks to push the pace whenever he gets the opportunity. He loves to take chances with the puck, and provides a good presence from the backend offensively with his size, hockey sense and puck skills.

The first thing you notice about Ristolainen is his positioning in the defensive zone. Whenever the play is along the half wall or around the blue line, he creeps up to the high slot and waits for his team to get possession of the puck so that he can join the rush. There are times when he gets caught and opponents have a small odd man scoring chance, but more often than not he does pick his spots quite well and is able to create an odd man rush up the ice for his team. Defensively, Ristolainen is physical along the boards, and maintains an excellent gap off the rush. He is very aggressive in the neutral zone, and does not give opponents a free pass to gain the blue line. He uses his stick quite effectively, and is able to knock away pucks on a consistent basis.

Ristolainen is a very good skater. He does not possess great top end speed, but he uses his edges so well to maneuver through traffic and carry the puck easily. He makes quick starts and stops to stick to opponents well in the defensive end, and does a good job of angling players to the outside and ensuring that they do not get a lane to the net off the rush. His feet allow him to look so smooth out on the ice and also allows him to do all the things that he does every game.

Offensively, Ristolainen is so poised with the puck on his stick. He will exploit holes in the neutral zone and carry the puck when given an opportunity, or make a crisp, tape to tape pass to his teammates to start the rush on a consistent basis. He has good vision with the puck and makes smart decisions with the puck time and time again. He also has a very good shot from the point, which allows him to be unpredictable in the offensive zone. He has slick hands, which he displays time and time again when he carries the puck up the ice through defenders. Ristolainen has proven to be a very effective player at the professional level already in Finland.

Max Domi

Center – London Knights (OHL)
Born March 2 1995 – Toronto, ONT
Height 5.09.25 - Weight 197 - Shoots L

Games	Goals	Assists	Points	PIMS	+/-
64	39	48	87	71	+33

Max was selected in the 1st round, 8th Overall by the Kingston Frontenacs in the 2011 OHL Priority Selection Draft out of the Don Mills Flyers Minor Midget program. Max was arguably the best player available in the draft, however fell due to potential NCAA commitments. After a little negotiating, Max was traded to London from Kingston and would begin his career with the Knights on schedule. Max is the son of former NHLer Tie Domi. While he possesses the grit and resiliency of his father, he plays a much more skilled dynamic style of game fueled by his physical talents and high level hockey sense.

Max instantly became a contributing player on a veteran London squad. Max was a productive player in his rookie season and was one of the most talented rookies in the entire CHL. Max not only produces points but he comes through at the most critical moment in the game. London had many come from behind victories and often, when the game was on the line, Max elevated his play to a higher level. Domi handles the puck extremely well and shows great shiftiness. He is extremely difficult to contain because he is an excellent skater. He accelerates quickly, changes directions on a dime and can fly around the ice.

Along with his skating he is built very solid. He's not a big player but possesses exceptional core strength allowing him to absorb contact and keep going. Max has an excellent shot which is very accurate and he is capable of finishing consistently. He displays excellent vision and while he's more than capable of putting the puck in the net, he can create and set up scoring chances in ways that few other prospects can. In terms of improvements, Max can get into slumps where he occasionally tries to do too much and gets caught turning over some pucks in the grey zones. We see Max as a sure fire first rounder. While his size may drop him on some teams draft boards, it wouldn't be out of the realm of possibilities for Max to find his way into the top 10 or 15 picks.

Max projects to be a skilled top six forward at the next level who has a very high potential ceiling. He has proven to us over many viewings that he excels in clutch situations. Max will also benefit from his character, which is highly regarded as an individual.

Bo Horvat

Center – London Knights (OHL)
Born May 4 1995 - Rodney, ONT
Height 6.00 - Weight 206 - Shoots L

Games	Goals	Assists	Points	PIMS	+/-
61	33	28	51	29	+

Horvat was selected 1st Round, 9th Overall out of the 2011 OHL Priority Selection Draft by the London Knights out of the Elgin-Middlesex Chiefs Minor Midget program. Bo really impressed us in Minor Midget and we were impressed with this pick. There was no question of his work ethic, but there was a question if he would be able to produce at the OHL level. While it took him a little bit to get rolling, he put up a respectable 30 points as a 16 year old playing a bottom six role with the Knights. Horvat really became more known after he was named captain of Team Ontario at the World Under 17 Challenge and put on a great performance putting up more than a point per game. He really hit his stride as a hard working two-way player who played with maturity beyond his years. While quiet on the scoresheet, his forecheck, defensive play and competitiveness is evident in every shift.

With a new season came new responsibilities for Horvat this year. He started out in and out of the top six but it didn't take long for him to establish himself as a game by game top six all situations kind of guy. Bo isn't a flashy player although he is capable of making a few moves and beating defenders. He also has tremendous focus and hand/eye coordination, making him very dangerous in the goal area. He has excellent positioning in all three zones, but in the offensive zone he moves around from the front of the net, and sliding off to the side setting up for scoring chances. He has an excellent forecheck and competes hard in corners, along the walls and wins more battles than he's expected to. Bo is also very solid defensively. He blocks shots and gets in lanes on the penalty kill. Defensively, he hurries back in transition and can break up scoring chances. He is smart, positionally, and isn't afraid to go down low to compensate for a defensive mistake by a teammate.

Bo's game projects extremely well for the pro level and he has the size closely similar to a power forward. Skating has always been an area of Horvat's needing improvement. He has shown improvement over the last two years, but will need to get even better to reach his potential at the pro level. Bo is a safe pick in the 2013 NHL Entry Draft and is secure in the first round. It wouldn't be a shock to see him creep into the top 10 or 12 players selected in this draft.

Alexander Wennberg

Center – Djurgarden (SWE-2)
Born Sep 22 1994 - Stockholm, Sweden
Height 6.01 - Weight 190 - Shoots L

Games	Goals	Assists	Points	PIMS	+/-
46	14	18	32	14	+12

Wennberg is a strong two way forward who displayed a very good combination of size, skill and hockey intelligence at the 2013 World Junior Tournament. He initially started on the 4th line, but played his way up onto a top six role with his consistent effort.

Wennberg is most effective along the walls. He is strong on his skates and wins a lot of battles for loose pucks. He uses his edges well to quickly change directions to buy himself some time to make a pass or to walk towards the slot and get a scoring chance. He is at his best when playing a physical game and outworking opponents to win battles and be tough to play against in front of the net. Wennberg has very good vision, and manages the puck well. He does not make poor decisions with the puck and allows the play to develop before making a pass. He is able to protect the puck with his frame and drive to the net when possible. He has a good release to his shot, but will need to shoot the puck more to add another dimension to his game.

Defensively, Wennberg plays with his head on a swivel and is very aware of the situation out on the ice. He puts himself in a good position to take away plays from the point. He is tough to play against because of his physical game, and consistently outworks opponents without the puck to help his team win games. Aside from his work with his body, Wennberg thinks the game well, and plays with good confidence and makes quick reads. Teams will definitely be interested in Wennberg's solid overall game. He may not have elite offensive abilities, but his intensity and physical game makes up for it. He has some work to do for his overall game, but he has had good success offensively this season while playing on Djurgarden's men's team. He should be used to the speed of playing with older players, which puts him in a good position to succeed in the future at the NHL level.

Quotable: "I got my first chance to speak to Alex at the combine. It was easy to see why I got several rave reviews about his interviews from scouts. He was as impressive as any player I have spoken to. On the ice I always look for smart players and Wennberg is a very intelligent hockey player." - Mark Edwards

Valentin Zykov

LW - Baie-Comeau Drakkar (QMJHL)
Born May 15 1995 - St. Petersburg, RUS
Height 5.11.75 - Weight 209 - Shoots R

Games	Goals	Assists	Points	PIMS	+/-
67	40	35	75	60	+29

Zykov made his debut in North American soil in 2012-2013 and has been a terrific goal-scoring force in QMJHL with 40 goals scored in his rookie season. The St. Petersburg native uses his frame well to protect the puck and create time to maintain puck possession in favor of his team. He is already one of the strongest players in the league in 1-on-1 situations and we have rarely seen him get knocked off the puck when he uses this asset along the boards. He loves to crash the net and is not afraid of getting hit while doing so. Zykov also possesses tremendous puck control and has made some magnificent plays in tight spaces. An unpredictable player to follow in coverage, Zykov has shown his hands beating goaltenders and defenders displaying a great skill set and nice elusiveness. He has natural goal scoring instincts, shooting on net whenever he can and positioning himself in goal scoring areas when he doesn't have the puck. He has a rocket of a shot which possesses excellent accuracy.

Valentin Zykov is not a selfish player and will make good use of teammates when cycling the puck or working around the net, although his playmaking abilities are not near his goal scoring abilities. He will hit players on the forecheck and get physical in front of the net, being an active part of scrums. Although he has tons of skills, Zykov can play an aggressive, gritty game when he is asked to, which shows a lot of versatility in his game. Defensively, he understands his role and will rarely be caught cheating, playing strongly on the wall, winning the important battles and hardly causing any turnovers at his own blue line. We like the intensity, consistency and character he has shown in our multiple observations of him. He has rarely backed down from a challenge and was a big time performer in important moments for Baie-Comeau this season,

Valentin Zykov's speed has improved as the season progressed, but it's still hindering him in defensive coverage at times. The fact that he's been having such success without having any high end speed speaks volume about the his natural talent with the puck, goal-scoring instincts and defensive awareness. Skating should be something Valentin Zykov gets as his legs get stronger and when he gets that speed, he'll be something special.

Zachary Fucale

Goalie – Halifax Mooseheads (QMJHL)
Born May 28 1995 – Laval, QC
Height 6.01 - Weight 181 - Catches L

Games	Wins	Losses	G.A.A	Save %	SO
55	45	5	2.35	0.909	2

Zachary Fucale stands at 6'1", 181 pounds giving him a fairly decent size for a goaltender. He plays a standard butterfly game, focusing on covering his angles and trying to stop more pucks by doing less. What separates him from others is his mental toughness.

Zachary is unshakable, nothing seems to get into his head in a hockey game. His composure is always disarming. He forgets a bad goal quickly, doesn't lose his focus when players crash his net, impressively keeps the same level of focus whether he receives 15 or 45 shots and just never seems to have mental fatigue even when playing back to back games. One thing we really like about him is the way he can control his emotions and make the key save when games are on the line. He just has that quality that clutch goaltenders have.

Fucale is not an aggressive goalie, limiting the movements he needs to do to make a save, he will rarely overreact when making his lateral movements, showing tremendous control on his body when moving. He is a really smart goalie with great anticipation; always finding a way to track pucks and knowing what are the puck carrier's options, helping him getting in position in time in the case of a pass. A great athlete, Fucale is a very quick goalie. We have seen him make saves on superb post-to-post movements displaying his flexibility. His legs are strong and quick helping him in the rebound control area and in his lower-net coverage.

We would like to see Fucale be more aggressive as his calm and cool can be his own worst nightmare exemplified by staying too deep in his crease which forces him to make reactionary saves instead of coming in front of his crease and letting the puck touch him. Some pucks might get through because of that bad habit, making him look vulnerable at times. Fucale also needs to get a better catching glove, sometimes putting it too low. We also feel his reflexes with both hands need to get better for professional hockey.

Madison Bowey

Defense – Kelowna Rockets (WHL)
Born April 22 1995 – Winnipeg, MB
Height 6.00.75 - Weight 195 - Shoots R

Games	Goals	Assists	Points	PIMS	+/-
69	12	18	30	75	+41

Bowey is a dynamic defenseman who has continued to improve his overall game. His best asset is his skating abilities, which he uses with and without the puck to be a force for the Rockets every game. In an interview with HockeyProspect, Madison has acknowledged that he has been focusing on playing a more solid game in his own end this season and letting the play come to him, which he has definitely improved on since last year. Offensively, Bowey is very fun to watch. He loves to skate with the puck and add another dimension to the Rockets' transition attack with his speed. He moves the puck very well when necessary, and is an important piece to their power play. Bowey sees the ice well and identifies open lanes and makes very good back door passes. He takes some risks at times that does not always pay off, but they are rarely terrible mistakes that result in great scoring chances for the other team. Bowey is mobile along the blueline, and makes it difficult for opposing forwards to cover him because he could move laterally or move down the boards with the puck in a hurry. He has so many options due to his speed, that opponents are half a step late in trying to read what his next move will be.

Bowey's game without the puck has come a long way from the start of the season. He does not chase the puck as much as he did, and lets the play come to him instead. He has done a great job in playing between the dots instead of trying to land big open ice hits and getting caught out of position. He still likes to take chances in the neutral zone to create turnovers and start a transition the other way, but he takes low risk, high reward gambles. He is strong along the walls and has a bit of an edge to his game, and is not afraid to get into an opponent's face and make it difficult to play against him. The aspect of his game that is fun to watch is that he plays with such a great level of energy. Even when he may be playing his 3rd game in 3 nights, he plays with the same enthusiasm consistently and it looks like he really enjoys playing the game. He back checks hard if he is ever caught in a bad position in the neutral zone, and quickly jumps into the play when he sees a lane that he can attack. He is hard to ignore when he is out on the ice, and will surely be a fan favorite wherever he goes.

Darnell Nurse

Defense – S.S. Marie Greyhounds (OHL)
Born February 4 1995 - Hamilton, ONT
Height 6.03.5 - Weight 205 - Shoots L

Games	Goals	Assists	Points	PIMS	+/-
68	12	29	41	116	+15

Darnell was picked by the Sault Ste. Marie Greyhounds and he was the top defenseman selected out of the 1995 born group of players at the 2011 OHL Priority Selection Draft. Darnell struggled a little out of the gate with high expectations as a 16 year old. As the season went on things started to fall into place but it really wasn't the rookie season most were expecting from Darnell. Fortunately as he went into Team Canada's U18 Ivan Hlinka camp he showed exactly how much he improved playing an important part in Canada's Gold Medal win.

Nurse is the prototypical shutdown defenseman in the OHL. He is big and can play a mean and nasty style of game punishing opponents in the corners and in front of the net. Nurse works to win battles along the boards and thrives pushing forwards off the puck with a strong physical compete level. Darnell hammers forwards in front of the net and is very effective at allowing his goaltender to see most shots from the point. He also shows a willingness to block shots and excels on the penalty kill setting up strong positioning and utilizing an active stick to disrupt passing lanes. Nurse is a strong skater and can quickly close gaps on rushing forwards crossing the blue line. Nurse shows confidence skating with the puck out of the defensive zone and has the ability to evade pressure with his feet. He generally makes smart outlet passes but needs to work at touch and precision allowing his line mates to receive passes in stride.

Darnell began to show some improvement in his offensive game as the season progressed and he was started jumping into the rush and contributing offensively. He needs to continue to work at improving the accuracy of his shot from the blue line, but has a decent wrist shot. He also shows great leadership qualities on and off the ice and works well with his teammates earning an assistant captain letter in only his second season in the league. Nurse is usually effective at puck moving and creating space for his line mates to work. Darnell has shown a willingness to drop the gloves from time to time and will stand up for his teammates.

Nurse struggled a bit in this year's playoffs and had trouble with his decision making. He got away from playing a strong defensive first game. Darnell showed enough however over the course of the season to remain a first round pick in the 2013 NHL Draft. He will be the key player on the Greyhound blue line next season with high leadership expectations for a younger OHL club.

Josh Morrissey

Defense – Price Albert Raiders (WHL)
Born March 28 1995 – Calgary, AB
Height 5.11.75 - Weight 186 Shoots L

Games	Goals	Assists	Points	PIMS	+/-
70	15	32	47	91	+14

Morrissey is a poised, puck moving defenseman who has quarterbacked the power play for Prince Albert for the last 2 seasons. He has a solid overall game, and while he may not be the biggest player, he will catch opponents with their head down in the neutral zone whenever he gets the opportunity. No matter how much pressure Morrissey may face when he has the puck, he always seems to find a way to either calmly skate it out of trouble, or quickly spin away from an opponent and make a laser beam, tape to tape pass to his forward to start the attack. He possesses very impressive vision on the point, and time and time again seems to be able to make difficult passes and threads the needle to go cross ice for good scoring chances. Not only does he have elite passing ability, he is able to read the play quickly and take advantage of any mistakes opponents make or be creative with the puck. He has a good shot from the point that he could use more. He walks the line with ease, and keeps his head up to unleash his shot when he sees an open lane, or to make a pass if an opponent cheats to take his shot away.

Defensively, Morrissey gives opponents very little room to work with. His skating abilities allow him to cover a large area, and his gap control is excellent off the rush. He has a good stick to knock away passes and to take away passing lanes. He does not chase the play, and looks calm under pressure. He also forces opponents to keep their head up and enter the neutral zone with caution because of his ability to step up and land good open ice hits. He quickly sees an opportunity to dish out a hit, and closes the gap in a hurry. The one area of improvement for Morrissey would be his strength. He has a hard time maintaining body position against bigger opponents in the slot, and may have a hard time tying up bigger and physically mature players at the pro level.

Morrissey's consistent level of excellence on the ice could allow his name to be called in the first round of the NHL Entry Draft. It is rare to find a defenseman of his age who is can make such an impact with the puck while not sacrificing his defensive game at all. Teams will have to wait a few years until he could be ready to play in the NHL, but with the proper development, Morrissey can surely turn into a valuable top four offensive defenseman one day.

Samuel Morin

Defense – Rimouski Oceanic (QMJHL)
Born July 12 1995 – Lac-Beauport, QC
Height 6.06.25 - Weight 202 - Shoots L

HOCKEYPROSPECT.COM

ROUND ONE #18

Games	Goals	Assists	Points	PIMS	+/-
46	4	12	16	117	+10

At over 6'6" and 202 pounds, Morin is an intimidating force on the back end. He improved his footwork this year, thus making it easier for him to play an aggressive, mean and physical game. You know it will hurt to go in a battle down-low with the big defenseman. He will pin you to the board easily and use his long reach to eliminate time and space from skilled players. He got over 100 penalty minutes this season, while he should cut down on undisciplined penalties. He was involved in many scrums, roughing situations in front of the net and fights, displaying his physical side well. He executes well the position game defensively, he blocks a lot of shots and covers a lot of space in slot coverage and he chooses the right moments to press the opposition most times showing good defensive hockey sense. He skates with long strides, making him a good forward skater. He has above-average puck control and agility offensively for a big man. He doesn't hesitate to be aggressive on the pinch, shows great confidence controlling the puck at the blue line and possesses a quality, low wrist shot with good accuracy.

Like most 17 year old defensemen his size, Samuel Morin still has a lot to improve before playing in the big league. Backward skating and gap control are still issues for him although it has progressed nicely in 2012-2013. He still has a hard time dealing with explosive skaters when they come out wide on him because he lacks backward speed and lateral mobility. Acquiring better explosiveness and overall skating abilities will help him play an even more aggressive game in all 3 zones. We would also like to see him take fewer undisciplined penalties, Morin has put his team in trouble more than once during the season with these. He still needs to put some pounds on to fill in that frame completely. With the size, mean streak and surprisingly good offensive potential he has, Samuel Morin is surely an interesting project for this year's draft.

Quotable: "Morin has come a long way since last year, he is nastier and more confident with the puck. Still does have occasional brain cramps that make you scratch your head but his upside is as high as any defensemen from the QMJHL. It's rare to see 6'7 defensemen has mobile as this kid." - Jerome Berube

Anthony Mantha

Right Wing – Val d'Or Foreurs (QMJHL)
Born Sep 16 1994 – Longueuil, QC
Height 6.03.75 - Weight 190 - Shoots L

HOCKEYPROSPECT.COM

ROUND ONE #19

Games	Goals	Assists	Points	PIMS	+/-
67	50	39	89	71	+21

Anthony's biggest strength is his shot. He can release from just about anywhere in the offensive zone and create a scoring chance with it. It is very hard, quickly released and he has an amazing accuracy with it and is able to put pucks on net with the intention to create a rebound for teammates. Mantha uses his long reach well to get around players, he has good puck handling skills, but he is not the kind of player that will try to get through players with slick one-on-one moves. He will use his puck handling skills and good skating abilities to cut in the slot, delay plays and change his angles before taking a shot. We like to see him use that frame to cut to the net and be aggressive. We would also like to see him throw the body more often.

Anthony Mantha is one of the smartest players available this year in the draft. His shot is one of the reasons he gets so many goals, but his intelligence on the ice is also a huge factor. He seems to know where the play is going before most players. He finds soft areas in the offensive zone very quickly and by doing so always make himself a passing option for a teammate. He has a shoot first mentality, but is also a great passer and has shown some great playmaking qualities in many of our viewings. His hockey sense is also well displayed in the defensive zone, placing his stick in a perfect position to create turnovers when he pressures opponents, reads the play quickly and anticipates like few can. He always seems to be a step ahead of his opponents, even in the defensive zone.

As talented and smart as Mantha may be, one big setback is his work ethic. On some nights, Anthony Mantha will hit, back check, skate hard and win his 1-on-1 battles. However, in a lot of our viewings, he will rely on his talent and stay out of the play, easy to push of the puck in battles. The lack of competitiveness and character has been very worrying for us in our viewings of Mantha. He can also start cheating and stop caring about his own zone. He knows how to play well in his own zone, but doesn't always want to.

Mantha has tremendous upsides but also huge downsides, so he's a pretty risky pick for this year's draft. If the work ethic issues can be resolved, there are no doubts that with the shot and intelligence he has, Anthony Mantha can be a steady goal scorer in professional hockey.

19

Ryan Hartman

Right Wing – Plymouth Whalers (OHL)
Born Sep 20 1994 – West Dundee, IL
Height 5.11 - Weight 181 - Shoots R

Games	Goals	Assists	Points	PIMS	+/-
56	23	37	60	120	+29

Ryan is hands down one of the hardest working players available in this 2013 NHL Entry Draft. He was selected in the 5th Round of the 2010 OHL Priority Selection Draft out of the Chicago Mission U16 program. Ryan opted to join the U.S. National Development Program and he has done an outstanding job representing his country. He's not even eligible to be drafted until June of this year and he already owns a U17, U18 and U20 Gold medal for Team USA. He also posted a point per game or better at both the World Under 17 Challenge and the IIHF U18 Championships. Due to his late birth date, while many of his USNTDP teammates went on to be selected at the 2012 NHL Entry Draft, Hartman weighed his options and chose to join the Plymouth Whalers this season. Ryan was in tough heading into camp. Plymouth was loaded at forward with several NHL Picks. He started out on the third line, but worked tremendously hard. By the time the trade deadline came and went, Ryan was on Plymouth's top line contributing on a nightly basis.

What we like most about Ryan is how hard he works every shift, every game. He plays whistle to whistle and battles for every inch. He has a tenacious forecheck and forces tons of turnovers. He hits and despite his average size, he packs a lot of power in his physical game. He has also shown a willingness to drop the gloves from time to time. He competes hard in all three zones and will work defensively creating turnovers and ending potential scoring chances against his team. Ryan was one of Plymouth's go to penalty killers and did an excellent job getting in passing lanes and sacrificing his body to block shots. The only question for Hartman going forward is whether his offensive game will translate at the next level. He shows good instincts in the offensive zone and is capable of reacting quickly and staying patient with the puck. He has an above average shot and is capable of creating plays not just with puck skills and hands, but also going back to his work ethic and just wanting the puck more than the opposition. There's little doubt that Ryan will be taken in the first round of the NHL Draft. He's a very popular player among scouts and he is highly regarded for his character. While he projects to go in the late teens or early 20's of the first round, a team that wants him bad enough may not take a chance and take him earlier.

Curtis Lazar

Center – Edmonton Oil Kings (WHL)
Born Feb 2 1995 – Salmon Arm, BC
Height 5.11.75 - Weight 178 - Shoots R

Games	Goals	Assists	Points	PIMS	+/-
72	38	23	61	47	+25

Lazar entered this season with a lot of hype surrounding his game. His play without the puck was very impressive for such a young player, while his offensive game was starting to improve showing potential in his game to be an effective two way forward in the NHL one day.

The best attribute of Lazar's game is his play without the puck. He is always in such good position in his own end, and is very strong along the boards. He is always out on the ice in crucial defensive situations, and will positively impact the game in some way. He fearlessly blocks shots to help his team win games, and seems to be able to consistently be in the shooting lane. His coverage down low is very good, and displays good anticipation to be able to knock away passes and tie up opponents. Offensively, Lazar has a very impressive wrist shot. He has a nice quick release off the rush in speed. He is not much of a playmaker, and most of his offensive contribution will come in the form of goals and scoring chances. He is able to get into good position in dangerous scoring areas, and make himself available for passes. Lazar has a bit of work to do with his hands around the net, as he could further develop his scoring touch. He has also shown that he is a streaky scorer. He may go a long stretch of not picking up any point, then go on a long streak where he seems to score whenever he is around the net.

Lazar will have to be able to consistently put up points to be a more dangerous player as a pro. Lazar is by no means a slow player, but he does have some work to do in terms of his acceleration. It takes him a bit longer to reach his good top end speed, and it inhibits him from being a more dangerous player than he could be. Any team that is looking for a heart and soul, future captain will not have to look further than Curtis Lazar. He may not put up more than 50 points a year in his prime, but he is able to impact the game in more ways than just offensively. He plays the game with such a passion, that it will be contagious within the dressing room. If he can continue to play a 200 ft game while improving his strength and speed and chip in offensively, he will put up a long NHL career.

Adam Erne

Left Wing – Quebec Remparts (QMJHL)
Born April 20 1995 – New Haven, CT
Height 6.00.5 - Weight 210 –Shoots L

Games	Goals	Assists	Points	PIMS	+/-
68	28	44	72	67	+11

Erne has put yet another solid season this year in the QMJHL. He was a reliable force on offense for the Quebec Remparts as he improved his production from last year. He is not that dynamic but he does a good job exploding on the wing and cutting to the net. Erne possesses tremendous top speed and can make even the best defensemen look vulnerable. His feet are quick and they make him an agile skater, twisting and turning with ease on the boards. He won't hesitate to control the puck for extended periods of time and does a good job of letting it go at the right moment. Erne is a natural goal scorer with a quick release and one of the hardest shots in the draft. He showed great offensive hockey sense on multiple occasions, getting into a scoring position when teammates control the puck. Erne is dangerous around the net, his bread and butter all season long, crashing and feeding open teammates, trying the wrap around or simply jumping on rebounds.

One of the reasons why the words power forward are used when talking about Erne is because of his blend of grit and physical play. He can impose a nasty physical presence along the boards with his size and good motor skills. We have seen him absolutely destroy some of his opponents with punishing hits, whether they are in his own zone or on the forecheck, Defensively, Erne has progressed well, using great anticipation to play his positional game and physical intensity to make sure the puck gets out.

One of Adam's few weaknesses is his consistency. He can get away with a non-physical approach to his game in the Q by using his speed, good hands around the net and finishing touch to have an impact on the game. We feel it's a commitment he will have to make every night in professional hockey to be successful. Erne has been a favorite of ours in his last two seasons. His mix of hockey sense, physical ability and good hockey tools makes him a very valuable prospect in this draft class.

Morgan Klimchuk

Left Wing – Regina Pats (WHL)
Born March 2 1995 – Regina, SK
Height 5.11.25 - Weight 180 - Shoots L

Games	Goals	Assists	Points	PIMS	+/-
72	36	40	76	20	-1

Morgan Klimchuk enjoyed a big break out season this year for the Pats, who as a team really struggled. Klimchuk was able to put up solid offensive numbers all season long while taking care of his defensive game too.

The first thing you notice about Klimchuk is his speed and tenacity. He plays the game at such a quick pace, and is not afraid to get into corners and try to win battles for pucks. He is constantly moving his feet, and really uses his speed to his advantage. He can turn on a dime with the puck while maintaining full control, and is able to make quick starts and stops. Offensively, Klimchuk is difficult to contain. He uses his speed and puck handling abilities off the rush to get good chances, and in the offensive zone he has the special ability to be able to disappear and find open areas in coverage to unleash his deadly one timer from the high slot. He is dangerous off the half wall on the power play because he can skate to the net and place a perfect shot in just about any areas of the net. Klimchuk is fearless when he drives the net, and is willing to sacrifice his body for his team. He will likely not become much of a playmaker at the next level as his vision is limited.

An area of Klimchuk's game that he is improving is his work in the defensive zone. He is still working on his positioning and reading the play without the puck. It has improved steadily as he season has progressed, but he still has work to do to not be a liability as a professional. One encouraging sign of his defensive play is his willingness to block shots. Time and time again Klimchuk would dive in front of one timers from the point to help his team win. The combination of speed, heart and offensive abilities will be tough to ignore for teams drafting in the late first round. Klimchuk will see a ton of ice time with the Regina Pats next season, which will only help with his development. It is clear that he is more than willing to play without the puck and do anything for his team to win, and teams definitely cannot have enough of players like Klimchuk in their lineup.

Hunter Shinkaruk

Center – Medicine Hat Tigers (WHL)
Born October 13 1994 – Calgary, AB
Height 5.10.25 - Weight 181 - Shoots L

Games	Goals	Assists	Points	PIMS	+/-
64	37	49	86	44	-13

There were a lot of questions as to whether Hunter Shinkaruk could put up the same types of numbers with ex-teammate Emerson Etem moving onto the AHL this season. Sure enough, Shinkaruk was able to prove that last season was no fluke, and led the Tigers with his impressive offensive skills.

It is difficult to find a player who is as dynamic offensively as Hunter Shinkaruk. He plays the game at such a high speed, that teammates sometimes have a difficult time keeping up with him. He has very good hands that he is able to use to maneuver around opponents as he is skating at full speed. Shinkaruk has a good release to his shots that is able to fool goaltenders. He has the ability to consistently score highlight reel goals, and really make players around him look so much better. He is relentless on the forecheck and knocks opponents off the puck well.

Defensively, Shinkaruk has made some good strides in his game in that area of his game. He is good at getting into the shooting lanes of opposing defensemen, and is not afraid to block shots when necessary. He has also become a key contributor on the PK for the Tigers, and adds a dangerous scoring element for them. He still needs to work on his physical play along the boards and using his stick more effectively, but it is definitely a good sign to see him improve his play without the puck. It will be interesting to see how Shinkaruk will adjust to the professional level. He is able to get away with trying to get through opponents all the time at the junior ranks, but it will be tough to do so against much more mature players. He will have to develop a knack of getting into open areas to score to contribute to his team. His offensive talent is undeniable, but it will be interesting to see just how successful he will become.

Quotable: "He left me wanting more early at the U18 in Brno last year, but I was jet lagged as well, so I cut him a lot of slack. He got much better. You can't deny the points he puts up. I have heard a lot of talk about him from scouts this year. Seems guys are either really hot or cold on him or have him as a 1st round slider. I had multiple scouts tell me his interview with their team during combine week was not good." - Mark Edwards

Nicolas Petan

Center – Portland Winterhawks (WHL)
Born March 22 1995 – Delta, BC
Height 5.08.5 - Weight 165 - Shoots L

HOCKEYPROSPECT.COM

ROUND ONE #25

Games	Goals	Assists	Points	PIMS	+/-
71	46	74	120	43	+68

Nicolas Petan has been one of the biggest stories to come out of the WHL this year. An undersized centre, Petan came out of nowhere to lead the dominant Winterhawks offensively and burn opponents all year long with his elite offensive skills. Even as the season went along and more and more attention was given to him and his line mates, Petan continued to put up huge numbers and put himself in the talks of being a first round draft pick in the upcoming NHL Entry Draft despite his size.

Petan's best offensive attribute is his vision and playmaking abilities. He is so patient and poised with the puck, and waits for the perfect moment to make a quick pass for an easy goal. He seems to have a pair of eyes on the back of his head, because he made some unbelievable no look passes from behind the goal line to a teammate or passes off the half wall. His confidence with the puck has really made the difference in his game this season. Petan was also very impressive at finding open areas in the slot to score some timely goals. He also displayed very good stick handling skills and showed some nice elusiveness. Simply put, he could not be stopped this season.

The biggest concern with Petan is his lack of size. He has shown some weakness along the walls and for puck battles, but it is not for a lack of effort. He engages physically whenever he has the opportunity, and drives to the net for loose pucks as hard as anybody. He has shown that he can quickly turn away from opponents and make it hard to tie him up, but as a center he will have to match up with much bigger center's down low on the defensive end. If Petan can outsmart opponents with and without the puck to compensate for his size, he could have some big impact as a pro.

Quotable: "I really like Petan. I had a lot of people ask me why is Domi ranked higher? For me it's two reasons. First, Domi has a very strong core. Secondly, I think Domi helped his line mates more than he was helped. Petan is smart and skilled but I think his line mates helped him out as well. Regardless, he's a first rounder in my books. He's small but elite." Mark Edwards

Chris Bigras

Defense – Owen Sound Attack (OHL)
Born February 22 1995 – Orillia, ONT
Height 6.00.5 - Weight 186 - Shoots L

Games	Goals	Assists	Points	PIMS	+/-
68	8	30	38	34	+35

Chris was selected 2nd round, 41st overall at the 2011 OHL Priority Selection draft out of the Barrie Colts Minor Midget program. The Attack made a great pick in selecting Chris who improved at an alarming rate throughout his rookie season. Despite Owen Sound being one of the best teams in the Western Conference last year, Chris was used on the power play as a 16 year old and looked like one of the better young offensive defensemen coming up from his age group. What was really impressive came early on this season. Chris had greatly improved his defensive game and was extremely reliable in a shutdown role. He doubled his points total from last season, despite being used in a stronger defensive role.

Chris enters the 2013 NHL Entry Draft as one of the most well rounded defenders eligible for the draft. Chris sticks with his man very well along the boards and is rarely evaded even by the shiftiest of skaters. He moves very well in all directions and is extremely tough to beat in one on one situations. His positional play is generally strong, but he does have an occasional tendency to lose his positioning. This is something he's improved at throughout the year and is really our only concern defensively, besides Chris getting stronger. Offensively he was a lot more tame and selective in when he would use his puck skills. However, when he did choose to rush the puck he was very effective going end to end evading checkers. He is a smooth puck mover who makes intelligent decisions and rarely makes a mistake.

Bigras projects to be a player who isn't going to be a star in the NHL, but he's going to be an all game situations player. He won't be the #1 penalty killer, or power play quarterback, but he will be able to play both of those roles effectively in the NHL. He isn't projected to be a top pairing guy, but he would be a compliment to a team's top four. He's one of the most well rounded defenseman in the 2013 NHL Entry Draft.

Quotable: "Chris showed his strong offensive game in his rookie season. This season he really proved he could handle the big minutes against top forwards while still showing flashes of his offense. In my mind Chris is one of the most underrated defensemen in this draft." – Ryan Yessie

Emile Poirier

LW – Gatineau Olympiques (QMJHL)
Born Dec 14 1994 – Montreal, QC
Height 6.00.75 - Weight 183 - Catches L

Games	Goals	Assists	Points	PIMS	+/-
65	32	38	70	101	+0

Émile Poirier has amazed us with his speed, scoring multiple goals and creating chances going wide on defensemen. He is deceptive and will create space for himself. He can also undress defensemen with sweet one-on-one moves. He can stickhandle in tight spaces with ease and is also a natural goal scorer. He also possesses a great wrist shot and has good accuracy.. He has great hockey sense and sees his teammates really well in the offensive zone. With his soft hands and great passing skills, Poirier has no problems passing the puck through sticks and skates before reaching teammates.

Poirier is not only a gifted goal-scorer, but a very smart player, he anticipates quickly and is always a threat because of his speed and active stick. He takes away a lot of time for the opposition when they have the puck. He plays on the PK and is well served by his great anticipation and hockey sense, blocking shots and his position fairly well. He's started to hit with more regularity and win more battles than he did last year, he got stronger and improved his puck protection a lot. He also showed more aggressiveness, being more involved in scrums and even dropping the gloves to defend teammates.

Émile has progressed into a complete package for the next level and never stopped progressing this season. His biggest weakness is work ethic and laziness. Poirier will sometimes be seen cheating high in the neutral zone, while his team has not retrieved the puck in the defensive zone. From time to time, he will rely from on his skill set only and avoid hits with careless decisions. He will forget to do the defensive details that he does in other games, because he doesn't feel like it. He also has improved this area of his game this year, but is still lacking consistency from shifts to shifts. We feel that Poirier could have a big impact in professional hockey if he's able to get an irreproachable work ethic. His explosiveness and soft-hands are already above most players his age and with the progression he's had in his defensive game, we see him as a possible steal in the 2013 NHL Draft.

Kerby Rychel

Left Wing – Windsor Spitfires (OHL)
Born October 7 1994 – Tecumseh, ON
Height 6.00.75 - Weight 205 - Shoots L

Games	Goals	Assists	Points	PIMS	+/-
68	40	47	87	94	-21

It seems like Kerby has been a Spitfire forever, but he actually went through quite the journey to get to where he is now. Kerby was selected in the first round of the 2010 OHL Priority Selection Draft by the Barrie Colts. From there he was traded to the Memorial Cup Host Mississauga St. Michael's Majors where he spent the first half of his rookie season. Kerby was then delt to the Windsor Spitfires and finished his rookie season there. Due to his late birth date, he had one more year to go before he was NHL Eligible and he passed the time quite effectively. As the Spitfires were looking to reload their roster and get working towards a 2014 contender, Kerby was busy notching 41 goals as a sophomore OHLer.

You can really see Kerby's father Warren's influence in his physical play. Warren was always known as a hard working player and Kerby has seemed to learn from that. He finishes his checks very hard whenever possible and generally played his best games on the bigger stages. Along with his physical play, Kerby's best asset has to be his shot. He's not a fancy player who will stickhandle around opposing players. You won't see many highlight reel goals from Rychel. What you will see is a well positioned forward who constantly seems to be in the right spot with a lethal release allowing him to post back to back 40 goal seasons. Kerby is also willing to drop the gloves and has faired moderately well. While Kerby looks like an NHL player it seems the biggest gap is what he is projected to be. His shot suggests he could play a second line power forward type of role. His energy and board play suggests he can play as a third pairing.

Whoever selects Rychel will look for him to improve his skating ability and become that true second line power forward who can play physical and put the puck in the net while having a third line grinder as the safety net if he doesn't pan out the way they expect. On what should be a more improved team Kerby will continue to be the go to guy for the Spitfires, but can make the jump to the AHL for the 2014-2015 season thanks to his late birth date.

Frederik Gauthier

Center – Rimouski Oceanic (QMJHL)
Born April 26 1995 - Mascouche, QC
Height 6.04.5 - Weight 214 - Shoots L

Games	Goals	Assists	Points	PIMS	+/-
62	22	38	60	26	+22

Perhaps Gauthier lived in the shadows of other QMJHL rookies this season, at least on the score sheet, but he managed to put together a solid performance throughout the year. When talking about Gauthier, the one word we continually go back to is intelligence. He displays it in all phases of the game and reading the play extremely well. He knows where to position himself to be effective and showed to be one step ahead of his opponents on numerous occasions. If takeaways were to be counted by the QMJHL, there is no doubt you would find Gauthier's name at the top. He creates many turnovers in the defensive and neutral zone with his long reach and more specifically his awareness.

His play on defense and the penalty kill was stellar; his positioning was excellent and he did a good job using his big body defensively. His play with the puck is also very good, but not near the top regarding offensive contribution. Gauthier has all the basics covered with solid hands, a strong wrist shot and again, good hockey sense that allows him to make the right decisions and set up good plays. He likes to cycle the puck in the offensive zone and he protects the puck well with his body and solid hands. Gauthier is neither a dynamic playmaker nor a dangerous shooter, but he is very effective in his decisions as mentioned. In addition, he positions himself properly to be productive. We identified two areas of improvement while watching Gauthier play.

The first one is his skating. He moves well enough to play his two-way game effectively but he doesn't have the explosiveness required to apply additional pressure defensively or to power his way through the offensive zone. Second, he needs to make a greater use of his body along the board to punish opponents to maximize his potential.

Ryan Pulock

Defense – Brandon Wheat Kings (WHL)
Born October 6 1994 – Dauphin, MB
Height 6.00.5 - Weight 211 - Shoots R

Games	Goals	Assists	Points	PIMS	+/-
61	14	31	45	22	-7

Ryan Pulock was clearly the best player for Brandon this season. He carried his team all year long, but unfortunately it was not enough to get them to the playoffs.

In his third full year in the WHL, Pulock has developed into a very good offensive defenseman who provides a steady presence from the backend. Pulock may not be the fastest player on the team, but he can comfortably get around the ice to jump into the play or back check and cover for his mistakes. He is also good around tight areas to make quick starts and stops to stick to his man in coverage. Pulock's best weapon is his slap shot. He was able to record 102 MPH during a skills competition, and it is something that opponents really concentrate on to prevent him from using it. As the season progressed, opposing wingers stuck to him like glue to take him away as an option, which really hurt Brandon's offensive production. However, on the power play Pulock freely snuck down to the slot from the point, which presented him with some nice scoring chances. He was able to find open holes in coverage quite well, and picked the right times to jump into the play. Pulock is also a good passer, but it is something that he can improve on. There were stretches during the season when his hockey sense has come into question by our scouts because of the alarming number of turnovers he was committing. He has given up the puck less in the final 2 months of the season, but it is still something to keep in mind. Pulock has a solid frame, and he likes to use his body to try to separate opponents from the puck quite often. He plays a physical game and makes it tough on opposing forwards along the walls. He will catch a player with the head down in the neutral zone when given the opportunity, so opponents really have to keep their heads up. There are some questions to his play without the puck. He is not always in the right position, and he could do a better job with his stick to knock away passes and shots and to take away lanes. He needs to stay more patient and let the play come to him when he is in the slot.

Teams will definitely give Ryan Pulock a long look in the first round. He certainly has all the tools to be a successful pro, but he just has to improve his play without the puck and find ways to use his slap shot from the point.

Robert Hagg

Defense – MODO (SEL)
Born Feb 8 1995 – Uppsala, Sweden
Height 6.02.25 - Weight 204 - Shoots L

Games	Goals	Assists	Points	PIMS	+/-
28	11	13	24	24	+5

Hagg has shown us a wide array of play in our viewings. He has looking both outstanding and invisible in different games, and sometimes in the same game. He has excellent size but generally only seems to use it when he feels it's absolutely necessary. In the defensive zone he shows good positioning and knowledge of the play going on around him, but can get a little lazy and look uninterested resulting in unnecessary turnovers in his own end. He is capable of passing the puck from long distances but also effectively in the offensive zone. When he loses his focus, that is generally where the puck playing mistakes come.

One of Robert's strongest assets is his shot. He has a big blast he can unload from the point and usually chooses good shooting options. He gets so much power behind it, when it doesn't beat the goaltender generally it results in a nice big rebound for his forwards to jump on. Hagg is a player who we've felt all season long possesses the tools to be a great defenseman but lacks the mindset to be a great defenseman. Robert has the upside to be one of the best defensemen in the entire 2013 NHL Entry Draft. However his downside is just as drastic in the opposite direction. He will be a bit of a risky pick for this draft, but one that could potentially pay off big time.

Quotable: "This is a player that extends scouting meetings. I think he has top 10 ability but he only occasionally flashed it for me. I'd see one shift and love what I saw and then on the next shift he would leave me wondering what he was doing. His compete level was on and off. This was another player I had plenty of conversations about with NHL scouts. It seemed like most teams staffs had a wide range of opinions. Everywhere from top 10 to late 30's." - Mark Edwards

Quotable: "Early in the season my reports were negative, late in the year they were all positive." - NHL Scout

Olivier Bjorkstrand

RW – Portland Winterhawks (WHL)
Born April 10 1995 – Herning, Denmark
Height 5.10.75 - Weight 166 - Shoots R

Games	Goals	Assists	Points	PIMS	+/-
65	31	32	63	10	+38

Bjorkstrand came into the league as an import forward and quickly adjusted to the North American style of play. He mostly played on the 3rd line on a very deep team, but was able to make a good impact consistently and gave teams a nightmare in terms of matching lines every game.

The first thing you notice about Bjorkstrand is that he plays bigger than his size. He is very good along the boards and drives to the net hard. He may not be involved in many scrums after the whistles, but whenever he is out on the ice, he gives his full effort in tough areas. Another strength of Bjorkstrand is his skating abilities. He is so tough to tie up along the wall because he can make quick tight turns with the puck and buy his line mates some time to get open. He has very impressive acceleration and opponents have a difficult time keeping him to the outside.

Offensively, Bjorkstrand has very good overall skill. He possesses a good touch around the net, and a quick release. He positions himself well everywhere out on the ice, and constantly moves into open areas to receive passes. He is a good playmaker himself, and sees the ice quite well. Defensively, Bjorkstrand works hard in his own end without the puck, but still has work to do in regards to positioning. He has a tendency to lose track of his point man, and has a difficult time getting into shooting lanes and taking away passes as a result.

Quotable: "I liked him when I saw him last year and I have been impressed with him this season. The kid has an NHL release and he has impressed me with his compete level all over the ice. I like his scoring upside at the next level." - Mark Edwards

Quotable: "This kid will score a ton next season with Rattie gone." - NHL scout

J.T. Compher

Center – USNTDP (USHL)
Born Sept 8 1995 – Northbrook, IL
Height 5.10.5 - Weight 184 - Shoots R

ROUND TWO #33

Games	Goals	Assists	Points	PIMS	+/-
49	15	27	42	45	+12

JT was the captain of the U18 team and did an excellent job of leading by example with his intelligent, two-way play. He's a Swiss army knife of sorts, the type of player coaches are happy to put on the ice in any situation at any time of a game. Need a goal in the last minute? He's your guy. Need to keep the puck out of your net with the lead? He can do that too. Power play, penalty kill, 4-on-4, you name it. He can do it all with a consistently strong effort. He very rarely takes shifts off and plays the full rink.

His skating is excellent with swift acceleration and agility. With quick starts and stops, he can dart around the offensive zone and is very effective in a cycle. In flashes, he shows outstanding stick handling ability and creativity. He can be very deceptive. He has a nice selection of shots and shows good variety with a sharp wrister, good one-timer, big slap shot, and a nice backhand. He gets good lift on his shots in tight. He takes the puck to the net and goes to the dirty areas to battle.

His defensive game is very strong. He's aggressive on the back check, forcing turnovers in the neutral zone with good pressure from behind and acting quickly after regaining possession to catch defenders flat-footed going the other way. He helps his defensemen out whenever possible with an honest effort in his zone, an active stock, and shot blocking. He's a strong penalty killer with good positioning and is a threat to score shorthanded. Compher missed time early on in the season with injury, bringing up questions of durability with his sometimes-reckless play, but was a fixture in the lineup from the end of November onwards. His excellent all-around play makes him one of the safest picks in this draft class, and he has been consistent enough offensively this year to say that he could very well still be a solid offensive contributor at the professional level, though at this point that's not quite a sure thing.

Steven Santini

Defense – USNTDP (USHL)
Born March 7 1995 – Bronxville, NY
Height 6.01.5 - Weight 207 – Shoots R

Games	Goals	Assists	Points	PIMS	+/-
56	0	13	13	42	+6

Mean, strong, and sound at both ends of the rink, Santini is the best defensive prospect from the NTDP this year. A confident leader who brings it for big games and works hard on and off the ice, he rarely goes a shift without making a positive impression and can be iced comfortably in any situation.

A defense-first player, Santini makes life hell on opposing forwards, physically dominating those who come into his corner or try to camp out in front of the net. He makes very few mistakes against the rush and is difficult to beat wide, though he does chase the play from time to time when the opposing team get their offense set up. He steps up when he senses hesitation and can lay big, open-ice hits. He takes few penalties for such an aggressive player, but discipline is an occasional issue. Though he managed to go the entire year without scoring a goal, Santini's puck skills are actually quite good. He's not dynamic, and therefore not an ideal power play quarterback, but he has the ability to skate the puck out of danger and makes a good first pass. His shot is powerful and he keeps his head up when shooting, but his release tends to be slow and his accuracy is lacking. He's not particularly elusive against the forecheck but protects the puck well and shows good instincts under pressure. When he finds himself without an option, he's good about making the safe clearance. Excellent skating ties his game together. He has a powerful stride and is difficult to beat in tight with great edge work.

Santini projects as a top-quality, smooth-skating shutdown defenseman who won't be a liability with the puck. Santini is the type of glue player that helps teams win championships.

Quotable: "Had him really high on my list early this season. I thought he could post some offensive numbers but they never came. He's still a top 40 guy for me, I like the toughness, he moves the puck and can skate." - Mark Edwards

Michael McCarron

Right Wing – USNTDP (USHL)
Born March 7, 1995 – Gross Pointe, MI
Height 6.05 - Weight 228 - Shoots R

Games	Goals	Assists	Points	PIMS	+/-
49	11	18	29	166	+1

The hulking, Western Michigan commit is one of the more polarizing players in this draft class. He tantalizes with physical tools and displays of impressive strength but lacks enough consistency, particularly in regards to offensive ability, to label him as a top prospect. He puck-watches too much in the offensive zone when he should be using his size and strength to cause havoc and draw attention. It's easy to look at a big player and wish for them to play with more of an edge, but even if Michael was 5'10", he would still be too passive. For a player of his size, he loses 50/50 battles too often and doesn't pursue loose pucks with enough intensity. He has games where he relishes contact and takes it upon himself to hit to hurt, but needs to play like that all the time. He protects the puck extremely well along the boards but doesn't show much creativity with it and has a hard time penetrating into scoring chance areas.

Though he does well to take advantage of what he's given on the ice, he hasn't shown the ability to create his own space. His skating is average, he builds speed like a cruise ship with slow first steps but can eventually get going and is very difficult to stop when he does get to stride. Hockey sense is the big question here. He has the tools, but it remains to be seen whether he has the fundamental understanding of the game to be a successful professional. Adding a bit more mystique to his situation is the fact that his OHL rights are owned by London, who are lobbying to bring him on board for next season. The hard-nosed Hunters won't settle for anything but his best effort, and could be just what he needs to right his ship.

Quotable: "NHL Scouts I spoke to had Mike anywhere from an early second rounder to 3rd round or later. I Spoke to him at length at the combine and he impressed me with his honesty about his game. We spoke a lot about his team of choice next season, including his visit to London for game 5 of the OHL Finals. My gut feel after our chat is that he will be in London next season but I honestly feel that as of now it's still up in the air. His interview with me rose his stock a bit." - Mark Edwards

Laurent Dauphin

C - Chicoutimi Saugeenens (QMJHL)
Born March 27 1995 – Repenigny, QC
Height 6.00 - Weight 165 – Shoots L

HOCKEYPROSPECT.COM

ROUND TWO #36

Games	Goals	Assists	Points	PIMS	+/-
62	25	32	57	50	+0

In his rookie season in the QMJHL, Dauphin consistently had strong showings after strong showings. He had good offensive numbers with 25 goals and 57 points in 62 games played and led all players in the Q with 9 winning goals. First thing that really stands out in Dauphin's game is his puck control. A very creative puck handler, Dauphin has quick hands and is very unpredictable when he comes in front of an opponent. Dauphin has good top speed and he uses long strides to get that speed in neutral zone. He has a natural goal scorer's instinct, using his elusiveness to get those shooting lanes from the slot, especially on the power-play. Dauphin shoots a lot and doesn't wait for the perfect opportunity to let it go. He likes to cut aggressively to the front of the net, not afraid to get hit or roughed up when he does so.

A very smart player, Dauphin played in every situation for Chicoutimi. He is not particularly physical but rather he is willing to get hit to make a play. Responsible defensively, he will get into shooting lanes and pay a physical price to accomplish defensive missions. Dauphin will work twice as hard to correct a mistake that he or a teammate did, especially in the defensive zone. He showed tremendous work ethic and determination throughout numerous situations during the season, battling pain to stay in position or working through checks to get to the puck.

Dauphin's biggest weakness is his ability to accelerate. He lacks that extra step and the explosiveness to go around opponents. An improved explosiveness would make his 2-way game go from good to great. Another weakness of Dauphin is his poor use of his teammates. He has good vision and sees plays well, but with his skill level and elusiveness, he will sometimes try to do it all by himself which appears selfish. In his case, given his smarts, he's demonstrated that he can utilize teammates defensively but will too often choose to wait until he's in trouble or out of options with the puck before passing to a teammate offensively. Dauphin's pro potential is great, with more maturity and minor inherent weaknesses corrected. He could be a smart 2-way center or winger with natural goal scoring instincts.

Jacob De La Rose

Left Wing – Leksand (SWE-2)
Born May 20 1995 – Arvika, Sweden
Height 6.02.25 - Weight 190 - Shoots L

Games	Goals	Assists	Points	PIMS	+/-
38	6	6	12	31	+10

Jacob is a power forward prospect who needs to be physical to be his best. We have seen these games and he was impressive in them, but we have seen the games where he wasn't physical as well. He does a good job closing gaps and taking away time and space. He did show us some smart positional play and has shown some flashes of beating defenders 1 on 1.

We like the straight line skating and the work ethic he has shown us. He plays well in all three zones. Jacob is very aware of his need to work on his shot and his scoring ability. If can can improve in those areas going forward it will surely raise his stock.

Quotable: "I went into this season with a goal of figuring out Jacob's potential as a potential top 6 forward in the NHL. It took a while for me to see enough of him, but I think I got my answer. While he showed me some flashes of scoring skills, I'm not sure he has enough to give me confidence that they would translate well to the next level. I was a big fan of the kid last year and liked a lot of things in his game. I still think he has 2nd round value in this draft." – Mark Edwards

Pavel Buchnevich

Left Wing - Cherepovets 2 (Russia)
Born Apr 17 1995 – Cherepovets, RUS
Height 6.01 - Weight 176 - Shoots L

Games	Goals	Assists	Points	PIMS	+/-
24	8	15	23	36	-4

We saw him in Windsor last year at the U17 and again this year at the U18 in Sochi. While he didn't tear it up in Windsor last year he left an impression this year in Sochi. He is a highly skilled player who stood out on multiple shifts. He centred a line with Nichushkin and was veru good all tournament long. He has skill, playmaking abilities and has proven he can score. Although we have limited viewings he has made an impression. Heard some NHL guys talking about some concerns with him but we liked what we saw from him, especially at the U18. He needs to get stronger in order to progress to the NHL. His physical attributes are his weakness.

Quotable: "I watched him a few times in his home country and he impressed me in each game." - Mark Edwards

Shea Theodore

Defense – Seattle Thunderbirds (WHL)
Born August 3, 1995 – Langley, BC
Height 6.01.75 - Weight 178 - Shoots L

ROUND
TWO #39

Games	Goals	Assists	Points	PIMS	+/-
71	19	31	50	32	-24

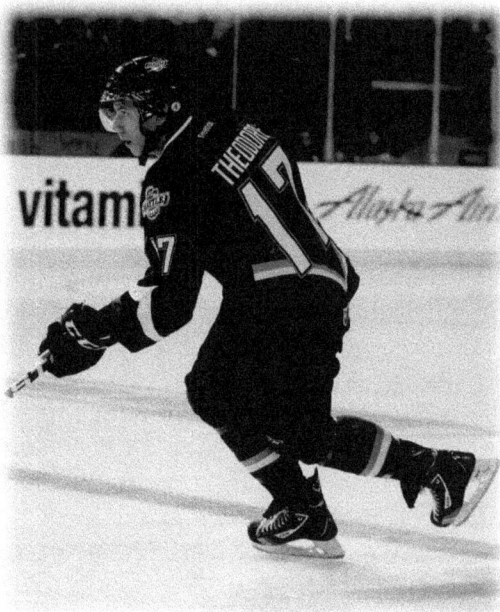

Teams will have a difficult time finding a defenseman who is as skilled with the puck as Shea Theodore in the upcoming NHL Entry Draft. He has the ability to go coast to coast and score a goal to change the momentum of the game, and provide a strong offensive presence from the backend.

Theodore is excellent at using his long reach to keep pucks away from opponents as he quickly picks up speed. He has the ability to quickly identify open lanes, and changes his direction in a hurry to drive to the net and forces his opponents to be caught flat footed. He can control the puck so effortlessly and even when he is skating at a very high speed, while keeping his head up to identify any open teammates. Theodore can also turn on a dime to get away from defenders, and buy his team more time to get open. He often stays on the ice for the entire power play for the Thunderbirds and does a very admirable job. He moves the puck quickly and accurately, but may give up a few turnovers throughout a game as he gambles and tries to connect on long stretch passes. Theodore is definitely a pass-first player who can improve on his shot from the point. His slap shot could have more velocity on it, while he could get them on net more often.

The biggest concern of Theodore is his defensive abilities. He has a tough time getting into proper position without the puck, and often gets caught sleeping in his own end. He has to be more aware of his surrounding, and know where he should be in certain situations. One factor of his poor positioning may be his ice time. He eats up a lot of minutes for Seattle, which may get him fatigued and affect his play. Theodore uses his good reach to poke pucks away and keep opponents to the outside on a consistent basis. The upside in Shea Theodore is undeniable. He could make a huge impact as an offensive defenseman in the league, but he will need to be better defensively to not be a liability out on the ice at the pro level. Coaches need to be able to trust him in any situation that they put him in. He certainly has all the tools to become an NHL defenseman one day, but his play without the puck and his ability to think the game will determine just how successful he can be.

Mirco Mueller

Defense – Everett Silvertips (WHL)
Born March 21, 1995 - Winterthur, SUI
Height 6.03.25 - Weight 184 - Shoots L

Games	Goals	Assists	Points	PIMS	+/-
63	6	25	31	57	-10

Mirco shows potential with his hockey intelligence with and without the puck, but his biggest flaw this year was the lack of physical play, particularly around the walls and in the slot. He was often pushed around far too easily.

Mueller's play with the puck is quite underrated. People rave about how good he is defensively, but often forget how good he is when the puck is on his stick. He makes excellent first passes out of the zone, and rarely tries to force a pass to his forwards. He takes his time to read the play, and if he does not have an outlet option, he softly puts it off the glass and into the neutral zone for his forwards to chase after it and try to win a battle for the puck. He receives a lot of time on the PP for Everett, and gets in good position on the blue line, and makes good, smart passes. Mueller could use his slap shot more to keep opponents on their toes however.

Defensively, Mueller is so difficult to play against. He has such a good stick, that opponents have a tough time doing anything when they are on his side of the ice with the puck. He will quickly knock away pucks, and keep everything to the outside. His gap control is very good, and he is able to give opposing forwards very little room because of his great skating abilities. Mueller possesses very good speed for his size, and has nice, quick feet to stick to opponents along the boards. The biggest improvement Mueller made in his game is his toughness. He will not be counted on to stick up for teammates anytime soon, but he looks very strong along the boards, and will not let anybody take him off his game with their forecheck. Mueller plays a very composed game, and will deliver good body checks when he gets the opportunity.

If Mirco Mueller continues to develop his overall game, there is an excellent chance that he will carve out a long, but quiet career in the NHL and be a player that can be depended on in every situation for his team.

Dillon Heatherington

Defense – Swift Current Broncos (WHL)
Born May 9 1995 – Calgary, AB
Height 6.03 - Weight 196 – Shoots L

Games	Goals	Assists	Points	PIMS	+/-
71	4	23	27	80	+25

Heatherington is one of the biggest risers for the upcoming NHL Entry Draft from the WHL. His defensive game has progressed steadily throughout the year, and is definitely one of the most defensively sound players available. He has size, grit and hockey intelligence that he uses on a nightly basis to shut down the best opposing forwards.

The most impressive aspect of Heatherington's game is his ability to read the play. He is very composed and lets the play come to him. He stays in good position in front of the net, and makes sure that he is always in between the puck and an opponent so he can intercept passes easily and not allow any scoring opportunities. He is very physical along the boards, and is hard to knock off the puck. He uses his size to his advantage, and keeps opponents to the outside with his long reach. He plays with an edge at all times, and will mix it up with opponents when necessary. Offensively, Heatherington makes solid passes out of the zone. He will never dominate a game offensively, but he does a good job of pinching when he sees an opportunity, and come down the boards to hold the puck and keep the offense going. He rarely takes risks with the puck, and ensures that he is able to start the attack for his team with a good first pass. An area of improvement for Heatherington would be his skating abilities. He is a good skater given his size, but he will need to add speed and explosiveness in his speed to keep up with speedy forwards at the pro level. He is constantly in solid position and uses his reach to force opponents to the outside in the WHL, but it will get much tougher when players are faster and bigger.

Heatherington is a type of player that every team would love to have in crucial defensive situations. He can match up with the best forwards on a consistent basis and give them a tough time when they have the puck. He is a very efficient player who has all the tools to be a successful pro one day with more development.

Jason Dickinson

Center – Guelph Storm (OHL)
Born July 4 1995 – Georgetown, ONT
Height 6.01.5 - Weight 179 - Shoots L

Games	Goals	Assists	Points	PIMS	+/-
66	18	29	47	31	+19

Jason is a very smooth skater and is able to generate a good level of speed when given space to carry the puck down the wing or up the middle. He works hard to play all 200 feet of the ice and can be counted on in the defensive zone either helping out down low or winning battles along the boards to get pucks into the neutral zone. Jason is constantly working to keep body positioning on the D side of the puck and thus is seldom caught out of position. He has solid recovery speed that helps combat any time he is out of position.

Around December, Dickinson noticeably started to really ramp up his physical play which carried over to the second half of the season. Jason was constantly finishing checks in both open ice and along the boards and showed deceptive strength knocking a number of bigger opponents off of pucks with ease. He is good at using his body to shield opponents from the puck and will drive to the net with speed when given space. He generally worked along the wall on the power play and possesses a very powerful wrist shot from the top of the circle when coming in off the wall. Dickinson was also an exceptionally strong penalty killer for the Storm and was great at getting into both passing and shooting lanes and he blocked a number of shots throughout the season. He struggled in the face-off circle when forced to take the draw and is much better suited playing the wing. The biggest issue with Jason is the lack of offensive consistency over the season. There were games where his offensive skills would be on full display and he would dominate defenders both on and off the puck, and then there would be games where we saw little to no offensive pressure.

If he could improve consistency and feature his strong offensive skills on a nightly basis he will become quite the prospect in the years to come. Jason is considered to have very good character and is a player who is knowledgeable about the areas in which he needs to improve. The high end, if he can show his offense consistently, would see him being a potential second liner in the NHL. Dickinson can be a reliable two-way forward who shows flashes of productivity.

Artturi Lehkonen

Left Wing – KalPa (SM-liiga)
Born July 4 1995 – Piikkio, Finland
Height 5.11 - Weight 163 - Shoots L

Games	Goals	Assists	Points	PIMS	+/-
45	14	16	30	12	+12

Lehkonen may not be very strong, but he is certainly not afraid to battle for loose pucks and get in on the forecheck. The problem is that he rarely wins these battles, and is often knocked onto the ice quite easily. He needs to really work on his strength level to come away with the puck more often, as he will have to be much more involved physically at the AHL or NHL level to be successful. One clear strength of Lehkonen's game is his speed. He has very good top end speed, and is able to get from point A to B in a hurry. As a result, he is so successful in the bigger rinks as his speed allows him to create more separation from opponents and utilize his good stickhandling ability as well. He can make quick stops as he is moving at full speed while maintaining control of the puck, which throws opponents off guard as they have to quickly adjust and take away time and space from him.

Offensively, Lehkonen loves to shoot from anywhere. He is not afraid to go to the net to sniff out any rebounds, but he needs to be in a better position at times to take advantage of opportunities around the net and provide a better screen for his teammates. He possesses very smooth hands, and shows them off in the neutral zone with speed. One area of concern of Lehkonen's game is his inability to find open areas in the offensive zone. He needs to read the play better and get away from coverage to set himself up to receive a pass for a quick scoring opportunity in the slot. Defensively, Lehkonen uses his stick more than his body, which is something he needs to address. He likes to take a poke with his stick and just skate by the opposition instead of laying a hit and try to knock an opponent off the puck for a quick takeaway. He uses his speed to take away time and space in the neutral zone, but could do a better job of creating turnovers. He is rarely involved physically if he does not see much of a scoring chance coming out of the play.

It will be interesting to see if Lehkonen can find some success offensively on smaller ice. His game is built for lots of space with his speed and stickhandling rather than the "North American" game that he will have to play at the AHL and NHL level. If he does not improve his strength and ability to find open holes in coverage, he will have a difficult time making any sort of an impact for an NHL team in the future.

Thomas Vannelli

Defense – Minnetonka H.S (HS-MN)
Born Jan 2061995 – Minneapols, MN
Height 6.02 - Weight 165 - Shoots R

HOCKEYPROSPECT.COM

ROUND TWO #44

Games	Goals	Assists	Points	PIMS	+/-
25	8	23	31	14	+7

Vannelli is a quick skating defenseman who loves to join the rush and provides a lot of offense from the backend. He looks so effortless as he skates around the ice and gives opponents a difficult time trying to handle his speed.

It is difficult to not notice the impact Vannelli provides in games on a consistent basis for his team. Opponents always have to be aware of him joining the rush and to create an odd man opportunity. He is able to make a seamless transition from defense to offense with his very impressive skating ability, whether or not he has possession of the puck. He is able to quickly recover if a turnover ever occurs and get back into his defensive position before a scoring opportunity occurs for the opposing team. He possesses good vision and makes good passes, but his passing could be a little quicker. He also has a hard shot from the point, but he needs to do a better job of hitting the net. He does not have elite stickhandling abilities to deke through opponents at the pro level, and will likely have to make an impact offensively by joining the rush and being a good PP player.

Defensively, Vannelli's skating ability really allows him to thrive. He can maintain a good tight gap and drive opponents to the wall and not give them a lane to the net and maintain good positioning along the boards so that they will not be able to get past him and make a play. Vannelli is able to use his stick very effectively and knock away passes time and time again. The one big issue of his game is physical play. Vannelli is not very physical, and will need to add that element to his game as he has a very good frame. He still has some bulking up to do, which may allow him to be a more physical presence on the defensive end.

Vannelli is committed to the University of Minnesota and will have a very good opportunity to develop his game in a program that has produced so many NHLers over the years.

Remi Elie

Left Wing – London Knights (OHL)
Born April 16 1995 - Cornwall, ONT
Height 6.00.5 - Weight 203 - Shoots L

Games	Goals	Assists	Points	PIMS	+/-
65	7	10	17	34	+7

Remi was selected in the 5th round of the 2011 OHL Priority Selection Draft by the London Knights out of the Eastern Ontario Wild Minor Midget program. Remi stayed close to home last season playing for the Hawkesbury Hawks of the CCHL Remi made the London Knights out of camp spending the majority of the season playing on the Knights fourth line due to the tremendous depth of the team. His only escape from this has been when an injury occurs or someone in the top 9 has been underperforming. Usually this would result in Remi being promoted to a higher line that game. This has affected his numbers making Remi one of those players you have to watch closely to truly appreciate his level of talent.

While we see Remi posting a big point increase next season, what he brings goes well beyond stats. Remi plays a great power game where he wins battles along the boards and provides a relentless work ethic allowing him to win more than his share of battles. He plays a very physical game and will finish his checks. He also battles in his own zone winning along the wall. He reads the play well and can break up potential scoring chances with a stick check or to separate an opposing player from the puck. What helps Elie be as successful as he has been in his first OHL season, is his hockey sense. Remi has the ability to read the play. He's a big player, who knows he's big and knows how to use his size intelligently to give himself an advantage. While he competes in all three zones, he shows offensive potential with his shot. He has a cannon of a shot which was used at different times this season on the point of the Knights' power play. Sometimes it takes him a little too long to make puck decisions, but he has creativity with his passing.

Quotable: "On the very first day of London Knights training camp I took one look at this kid and 'wow' was my first reaction. London is doing a great job developing Remi, just wait until some of the older Knights graduate and his ice time goes up. He's going to show his true potential then. Some NHL team is going to steal this kid." - Ryan Yessie

Andre Burakovsky

Left Wing – Malmo (SWE-2)
Born Feb 9 1995 – Klagenfurt, Austria
Height 6.01 - Weight 178 - Shoots L

Games	Goals	Assists	Points	PIMS	+/-
43	4	7	11	8	+3

Andre has been a product of the Malmo system ever since he played for the U16 team as a 14 year old. He worked up to the J18 and J20 receiving an impressive 10 game tryout with the men's league team which started when he was just 16 years old. Andre has participated in two straight IIHF World U18 Championships in 2012 and 2013.

He was also a gamebreaker for Team Sweden at the 2012 World U17 Challenge. Andre really jumped out to us at this tournament and we saw a player with a great deal of potential. Unfortunately since then he hasn't quite reached that level of play in our viewings. Andre displays very good playmaking ability. He is creative with the puck and makes his linemates better with his puck movement. He always finds a way to slip into scoring positioning but he forechecks hard battling for pucks and showing strong skating ability to get to the wall and the corners very fast.

While he has a decent shot, in our viewings he seemed to lean more towards passing and creating rather than finishing. There really isn't a glaring weakness in his game. We would like to see him get stronger but the concern seems to be with the consistency in which he shows these skills. While he's a well rounded player, there have been too many instances where he simply did not show up to games or was invisible for long stretches. The potential is there but the consistency needs to follow for Andre to truly reach his potential.

Quotable: "I remember first seeing Andre at the World U17 Challenge in Windsor, Ontario. He controlled the puck, and the offense for Sweden so effectively. At 6'1" I saw a truly promising prospect at this event. Unfortunately, since then his production and performance offensively has been rather disappointing in our viewings of him. I really believe whoever selects Andre will give him many opportunities to be successful and I hope he takes advantage of these at the professional level and once again shows why we saw true first round potential in Andre earlier in his career." – Ryan Yessie

Ian McCoshen

Defense – Waterloo Blackhawks (USHL)
Born August 5, 1995 – Anaheim, CA
Height 6.02.5 - Weight 207 - Shoots L

HOCKEYPROSPECT.COM

ROUND TWO #47

Games	Goals	Assists	Points	PIMS	+/-
53	11	33	44	48	+35

The smooth, Boston College-bound defenseman plays a seasoned game and is a calming presence on the blueline. He's a fluid skater, especially for his size. He lacks top-end speed but his positioning is so sound that he rarely needs to churn his legs. He has a long stick that he uses well to cover the rush and cover lanes in his zone. He plays with an edge, making it difficult for forwards to gain net front positioning on him, roughing it up along the boards, and lining up big hits when the opportunity presents itself. He's steady and relaxed on the penalty kill, maintaining a presence without chasing the play. He protects his goalie and teammates, coming to their aid after whistles. He will drop the mitts when necessary.

He has a good point shot that he's not afraid to use and can get the puck on net through traffic. When necessary, he makes the safe play from his end but can also carry the puck out or stretch the play with long bombs. He likes to join the rush and picks his spots well, and also pinches aggressively in the offensive zone. He can run a power play and brings the puck up ice well with good reach and hands, though he lacks the dynamic offensive ability to be a major point-producer at the professional level. He plays with a lot of poise but at times lacks proper urgency when pressured by a strong forecheck and can be forced into errors. McCoshen has tools to be a top four defenseman in the NHL.

Peter Cehlarik

Left Wing – Lulea Jr. (SWE-JR)
Born August 2, 1995 – Zilina, Slovakia
Height 5.10 - Weight 168 - Shoots L

Games	Goals	Assists	Points	PIMS	+/-
38	17	20	37	10	+20

Cehlarik is a big two-way forward who plays a smart game. He seems to be in good position consistently to make a play at both ends of the ice and uses his size to his advantage on a consistent basis.

Cehlarik has good hockey sense. He is in good position on the forecheck time and time again, and is able to find open areas out on the ice offensively. He is not very quick out on the ice, so this ability is crucial for him to be involved in the play on a consistent basis. He possesses a good quick release, and is not afraid to go to the net for scoring opportunities. Cehlarik could be a little more physical, but he does a good job of protecting the puck and using his reach to try to create turnovers in the neutral zone.

The biggest weakness for Cehlarik is his skating ability. He is not very quick out on the ice, and if opponents have a step on him off the rush, he has a very difficult time catching up to the play and making an impact. Once the puck gets by him, he can be eliminated from the play at times. If Cehlarik can work on his quickness, he could be a good defensively responsible winger at the pro level in North America one day who provides offense once in a while. He certainly has the size that NHL teams look for, and the hockey sense without the puck.

Quotable: "He is a kid that made an impression on me in Sochi. He worked hard, played smart and flashed a quick release on his shot. Made a few poor decisions with the puck on a few occasions but nothing crazy. He made up for it with a few great passes in a game vs Germany. - Mark Edwards

Nick Moutrey

Left Wing – Saginaw Spirit (OHL)
Born June 24 1995 – Toronto, ONT
Height 6.02 - Weight 208 - Shoots L

Games	Goals	Assists	Points	PIMS	+/-
65	16	27	43	44	+2

Nick was one of our favorite players to watch in Minor Midget and was selected in the first round 15th Overall at the 2011 OHL Priority Selection Draft by the Saginaw Spirit out of the York-Simcoe Express program. Nick played regularly on the fourth line as a 16 year old, getting brief promotions up to the third line due to strong play or injuries to other players. Nick really improved over the summer and was used primarily in a second line role. He displays great physicality and usually finishes his checks.

Moutrey is a surprisingly good skater for his size and gets around fairly quickly. He wins battles along the boards and works hard winning more than his share of battles. He is surprisingly creative and can beat defensemen one on one and possesses a strong shot. Nick isn't a flashy player, or a player who brings a lot of attention to himself but he works hard and shows a lot of tools that are intriguing to Nick's potential success at the pro level.

Nick has been pretty effective in his own zone getting in passing lanes, getting in front of shots and clearing the zone well. His final numbers were a little concerning to us considering how well he played and the amount of ice he received. He needs to continue to play his game on a more consistent basis.

Moutrey should be a lock a to be picked at the 2013 NHL Entry Draft. At his highest potential, Nick could become a second line power forward as he possesses a good shot, and intelligent positioning. However a more safer projection, but what could see him drop in lists is the expectation that Nick will develop into a bottom six forward who plays hard on the boards, wins battles, chips in a little offensively and uses his size.

Jimmy Lodge

Center – Saginaw Spirit (OHL)
Born March 5 1995 – West Chester, PA
Height 6.00.5 - Weight 166 – Shoots R

Games	Goals	Assists	Points	PIMS	+/-
64	28	39	67	28	+4

Jimmy was selected in the third round of the 2011 OHL Priority Selection Draft from the Toronto Titans Minor Midget program. Jimmy was able to crack the Saginaw lineup as a 16 year old.

However he was caught behind several talented veteran forwards and really played a limited role due to his lack of physicality, but he did chip in a little offensively.

Jimmy saw a huge increase in ice time, receiving a ton of minutes with the Spirit playing in every offensive situation with some very talented forwards. Jimmy displays outstanding skating ability especially for a 17 year old at his height. Jimmy has shown us some real flashes of creativity. He uses his size to protect the puck fairly well and has a strong shot. He also showed great urgency to get back defensively and was willing to get his stick in lanes and battles.

The biggest concern about Jimmy is his lack of physicality. He really struggles and sometimes disappears in the more physical games and had a tendency of being taken off his game if matched against a big defenseman who asserted himself on Jimmy. He also didn't come out of enough battles with the puck. Fortunately he's only 165 at 6'2" so he's very lanky and would greatly benefit from adding muscle as soon as possible. He needs to get stronger, he already knows how to use his size, and it's possible that after adding 20, 30 pounds of muscle he will become more comfortable and effective in the physical game.

Jimmy is a player we are sure will be selected at the 2013 NHL Entry Draft. He has the potential upside of a top six forward but unless he gets tougher and adds more sandpaper to his game, he's one of those players that has to reach that top six potential to make the NHL. Otherwise he'll need to add that toughness and muscle that could make him an effective bottom six player.

Quotable: "He played a very soft game last year and in minor midget. He has made progress in this area and showed scouts he could post some crooked numbers. In talking to other scouts, opinions were all over the map." - Mark Edwards

Michael Downing

D - Dubuque FightingSaints (USHL)
Born May 19 1995 – Canton, MI
Height 6.02.75 - Weight 192 - Shoots L

Games	Goals	Assists	Points	PIMS	+/-
52	3	20	23	107	+16

At Michael is a hard-working two-way defenseman with a mean streak and upside. He plays with great awareness, tracking the play with his head up and keeping his feet moving. He joins the attack frequently and intelligently. He wants the puck and wants to be a difference maker. His pinches are aggressive but sometimes ill advised. He's a rover on the power play, taking advantage of his strong skating, smart passing, and great point shot. He tries to get into the head of his opponents with questionable stick work and chirping. He loves to throw big hits and is willing to drop the gloves.

Overall, he needs to watch his discipline and temper his aggressiveness. He makes mistakes in coverage, especially in outnumbered attack situations, by forcing the issue instead of allowing the play to come to him. He's also guilty of taking needless, badly timed penalties. The big blueliner is headed to Michigan in the fall.

Quotable: "He got better as the season went on. He was not good early this season. He probably raised his stock late with improved play." - NHL Scout

Linus Arnesson

Defense – Djurgarden (SWE-2)
Born Sept 21 1994 - Stockholm, SWE
Height 6.02 - Weight 187 - Shoots L

HOCKEYPROSPECT.COM

ROUND TWO #52

Games	Goals	Assists	Points	PIMS	+/-
31	0	1	1	8	-1

Arnesson is a steady defensive defenseman who does an excellent job of keeping plays to the outside and limiting the offensive chances that opponents create whenever he is out on the ice. The best asset of Arnesson is probably his skating ability. He is very quick on his skates, and when you combine that with his size, opponents have a very difficult time in trying to get inside positioning on him off the rush. He has good lateral movement, and is able to keep up with opponents as they try to go wide on him. Along the walls, Arnesson possesses very quick starts and stops, which comes useful as opponents try to shake him off and get a lane to the net.

He is not particularly physical, but he has displayed good overall strength to fight off opposing forwards for loose pucks, and stay on his feet even when he gets hit. Arnesson is consistently in good position to take away dangerous chances in the slot. He does not run around in his own end, and plays a very composed game without the puck. Offensively, Arnesson will probably never really become much of a threat. His outlet passes are above average, but lacks creativity. He keeps it safe when moving the puck, and thinks about defense first whenever his team is on the attack. He does a good job of keeping pucks in the offensive zone by moving down the walls when he sees the opportunity, but he will not take a chance if he does not see a clear chance. He does not like to use his shot very much either.

Arnesson may not provide many points in his career, but he will be a valuable piece to any defense unit as all teams need a shutdown defenseman to rely on when trying to hold onto leads. The one positive aspect of his game is that because he is so dependable defensively, teams can put him out there in any situation and trust that he will keep the puck out of their net.

Pavel Koledov

Defense – Lokomotiv Yaroslavl-2 (VHL)
Born Sep 20 1994 - Novosibirsk, Russia
Height 6.00 - Weight 181 – Shoots R

Games	Goals	Assists	Points	PIMS	+/-
35	1	3	4	10	-1

Pavel played primarily in the VHL for Lokomotiv Yaroslavl-2 putting on a strong performance at the World Junior Championships for Russia bumping some talented defensemen from the roster and played well for Russia.

Pavel really impressed us throughout our viewings of him. His size is average at best but he's very reliable defensively. He is effective in one on one situations showing a good gap control and good balance between a willingness to use strength and his stick. He competes very hard down low and has the ability to stick with his man along the wall. He battles hard and wins in the corners a surprising percentage of the time. He also maintains strong positioning in the defensive zone on a regular basis. He was also strong on the penalty kill forcing turnovers and getting the puck out of the zone while under pressure.

Pavel reads the play quickly and effectively and will jump up and intercept passes and take the m the other way. He has effective skating ability that allows him to carry the puck up ice. He makes good decisions on the rush around carrying and passing the puck off. He displays good hockey sense and always seems to be in ideal positioning in all three zones. Pavel made a real impression on our scouts and could an a steal in the 2013 NHL Entry Draft.

Quotable: "The first time I saw Pavel in person was in Boisbriand, Quebec at the Canada/Russia Subway Super Series. Over the series I was extremely impressed with how well he handled some of the top Canadian prospects in defensive situations. He was surprisingly consistent and committed to engaging in physical situations. He was certainly in my mind one of the unsung performers for Team Russia." – Ryan Yessie

Connor Hurley

Center – Edina High (HS-MN)
Born Sep 15 1995 – Eagan, MN
Height 6.01.25 - Weight 174 – Shoots L

Games	Goals	Assists	Points	PIMS	+/-
25	15	28	43	8	+1

Connor has played the last two seasons for Edina High School proving to be a key offensive contributor for his school. He has also enjoyed stints with the U.S. National Team Development Program and finished the season playing with his brother on the Muskegon Lumberjacks of the USHL. Connor really jumped out at us in our early viewings of him. He is capable of doing so many different things in a shift. He handles the puck well and displays good vision creating offense for his team. He provides an excellent work ethic when he's on his game forcing turnovers regularly and displaying a solid physical game finishing his checks. Hurley has had a few moments of inconsistency where we noticed him taking a shift off here and there, but it wasn't a major concern.

Connor has the high end upside of a power forward who can play a second line role. However to reach that potential he has a long way to go. He is fairly lanky and needs to add a lot of muscle to his frame. He has certainly shown us clear top six offensive potential at times, but these have been flashes and they have not occurred on a consistent basis. Connor likes to pass the puck, but has a laser of a shot and needs to utilize it more often. A safer and more reliable projection would be to see Connor ending up as a third line winger who uses his size and shows flashes of offensive production. He also has provided a very steady two-way presence in viewings of him playing with the USNTDP and Muskegon. Regardless, Connor has a lot of potential at the top level and is committed to Notre Dame University this coming fall of 2013.

Quotable: "Connor really jumped out at me at the U.S. Select 17 camp. He plays a hard working game and has told us that he sees himself as a playmaker. I found this a little surprising because of how good his shot is. Connor might take a little more time than some prospects in this draft to develop, but should fill out and become a very good two-way prospect." - Ryan Yessie

Adam Tambellini

Left Wing – Surrey Eagles (BCHL)
Born October 31 1994 - Edmonton, AB
Height 6.02.25 - Weight 169 - Shoots L

Games	Goals	Assists	Points	PIMS	+/-
52	36	29	65	26	N/A

Adam is the son of long time NHL executive Steve Tambellini and the younger brother of former 1st rounder Jeff Tambellini. Adam plays the game at a very quick pace, and is a very impressive skater for his size. Tambellini is very dangerous in the offensive zone because of his size, speed and skill. He has good vision, a nice release and is able to do everything with the puck at a high pace.

Opponents had a very tough time containing him this season because not many players in the league can play the game at the same speed as him. Tambellini can easily drive to the net and score around the net because teams did not have a defenseman who could match him with size and speed at once. He can play in so many different areas on the power play because of his unique skill set. There were times when during the same game, Tambellini would provide the screen on the PP, then the next opportunity play on the half wall and be a shooter, and then play on the point to be a playmaker. Teams really had to create game plans around Tambellini to try to stop him on a consistent basis.

The big knock on Tambellini's game at this point is his lack of a physical game. He could provide a more physical presence with his size, but stays away from contact when possible. He is not very gritty, and is not particularly strong along the walls. He will need to add an element of toughness to his game and increase his work ethic in order to maximize his high end potential.

Quotable: "Always tough to rank players like this. I didn't see him live but Charles An saw him a few times. NHL guys mostly said the same thing, elite talent but needs to put it all together." – Mark Edwards

Nicholas Baptiste

Right Wing – Sudbury Wolves (OHL)
Born August 4 1995 – Ottawa, ON
Height 6.00.75 - Weight 189 - Shoots R

HOCKEYPROSPECT.COM

ROUND TWO #56

Games	Goals	Assists	Points	PIMS	+/-
66	21	27	48	44	-1

Nicholas is a player we've seen a ton of potential in, even before his OHL Draft season began. Unfortunately multiple shoulder injuries slowed his development that year. He was still selected first round, 6th Overall, by the Sudbury Wolves out of the Ottawa Jr. Senators Minor Midget Program. He is a very quick, agile player that is physical and puts great pressure on the forecheck. Baptiste's biggest asset as a player is his speed.

He possesses good hands and the ability to create time and space for himself to make a play. He has a great work ethic, battles really hard for the puck and can protect it very effectively on the wide Drive. He competes to get to the front of the net, cycles the puck really well and puts great pressure on the fore-check, making sure to finish his hits. His best asset is definitely his speed, as he is the fastest player on the ice most nights. He has some creativity to make plays with the puck, is not intimidated to go to the dirty areas and doesn't panic when he has the puck.

He needs to watch some of the turnovers trying to force passes at times. He also needs to hit the net with more consistency. Like many players he will need to get stronger so that he can become a forceful power forward with great speed and quickness. Baptiste is a sure fire pick in the 2013 NHL Entry Draft and it wouldn't be a surprise to us to see a team use a second round pick on him..

Quotable: "We had many internal discussions about when Baptiste was going to start playing to the expectations we had for him. He showed flashes late in the season. I thought he had some good games in Sochi." - Mark Edwards

Quotable: "Nick stood out to us in Minor Midget, but we were waiting to see him show his potential at the OHL level as a true NHL prospect. As the 2012-2013 season went on, Nick finally started to show his true potential." - Ryan Yessie

Tristan Jarry

Goalie - Edmonton Oil Kings (WHL)
Born April 29, 1995 – Surrey, BC
Height 6.01.25 - Weight 183 – Catches L

Games	Wins	Losses	G.A.A	Save %	SO
27	18	7	1.61	.936	6

Jarry has been a backup to goaltender Laurent Brossoit for the last 2 seasons, and has developed into a solid prospect for the upcoming NHL Entry Draft. Although he has a great team playing in front of him, he has been able to showcase his abilities and the potential to become a very good goaltender at the professional level one day.

Jarry looks very poised and confident when he is on the ice. He does not waste much energy flopping around the crease, but rather keeps his movements quite efficient. He has shown good athletic ability to be able to quickly move post to post and make some big saves when necessary. He can comfortably move around the net on his feet and get in front of the puck as opponents pass it around for a scoring chance. Jarry has also displayed good hands and the ability to catch any pucks and deflect away shot to the corner with his blocker. He could still work on his overall mechanics to kick away rebounds better or to give opponents less chances after the initial shot. Another intriguing factor of Jarry's play is his ability to look like he has been playing regularly whenever he gets the start. He does not look rusty at all despite the fact that he receives very limited minutes. He seems to be mentally focused at all times to play, and it could safely be assumed that he consistently practices hard.

It will be very interesting to see how Jarry responds to being the starter for the Oil Kings next season. Judging by his mental game this season, it seems that he will be solid mentally even when he has games in which he struggles and be able to carry on with his solid play throughout the year. Teams will be taking a bit of a gamble when he has played in such a limited amount of games, but it could be well worth it in the future.

Zach Nastasiuk

Right Wing – Owen Sound Attack (OHL)
Born March 30 1994 - Barrie, ONT
Height 6.01.25 - Weight 190 - Shoots R

Games	Goals	Assists	Points	PIMS	+/-
62	20	20	40	32	+21

Nastasiuk was selected the Owen Sound Attack's 1st round (20th Overall) selection at the 2011 OHL Priority Selection Draft from the Barrie Colts Minor Midget program. This season Zach got off to another slow start and just as he got going he went down with a shoulder injury missing most of October. Once he returned to the lineup, Zach started to heat up and only got better as the season went on.

He shows a great compete level along the boards and as he got stronger he began to win even more battles. He controls the puck well and can stickhandle around opponents. He is also a very strong puck protector and uses this ability very well to maintain control or get a little extra time to make a decision with the puck. He loves to shoot the puck and has a very quick reaction time around the net which was key to him reaching the 20 goal mark in his sophomore season with Owen Sound.

While he plays a power game in regard to protecting the puck, playing in the dirty areas, he's not overly physical and he rarely takes a penalty. Zach's penalty killing ability has greatly improved throughout this season. He's intelligent position wise and always gets his stick in the lanes. His quick reaction pays off here as well allowing him to clear the zone when his team is under pressure. He has also sacrificed the body to block shots. So the question is why is a player we regard so highly ranked as low as he is? It all comes down to his skating ability. While he shows the potential to be a very good two-way forward at the next level, he not only has to overcome his skating ability but he will have a very long route to get here. He has trouble with balance, stumbles regularly and has trouble keeping up with the play, not because his talent doesn't allow him to, but because his skating isn't strong enough at times for him to be effective in high speed back and forth action. This needs to be the superior focus in his development process as it will likely hold the key to whether or not he can play at the NHL level. We would not be the least bit surprised to see a team who feels that his skating can be easily corrected to select him late in the first round. We hope he can overcome his skating because he has all the other tools to make him a successful player at the next level.

Viktor Crus Rydberg

Center – Linkoping Jr. (SWE-JR)
Born March 21 1995 – Vaxjo, Sweden
Height 5.11 - Weight 190 - Shoots R

Games	Goals	Assists	Points	PIMS	+/-
35	12	23	35	24	+15

Though he possesses outstanding two-way ability, Crus Rydberg is still very inconsistent. He has whole games where he's invisible, and turns in dominant performances in others. He's an excellent skater with great straight-line speed that can turn on the jets to get behind a defense. He carries the puck up ice with poise at high speed to back off defenders and create space.

He's good in the cycle game with agile stops and starts, and an excellent passer in all situations. He has a shot-first mentality with hard, accurate one-timers, snapshots, and wrister shots. He back checks hard and plays physical in his zone. He shows an active stick while defending to take away lanes all over the ice. His defensive coverage is overaggressive at times, but earnest. Crus Rydberg is an excellent talent, but needs to find a way to bring his A-game every night.

Quotable: "Viktor was maybe the most pleasant surprise of any player we saw at the Four Nations Cup. He didn't come in with a big reputation but he showed his potential NHL upside through skating, work ethic and great play in all three zones." - Ryan Yessie

Ryan Kujawinski

Center – Kingston Frontenacs (OHL)
Born Mar 30 1995 – Iroqouis Falls, ONT
Height 6.01.5 - Weight 204 - Shoots L

Games	Goals	Assists	Points	PIMS	+/-
66	17	31	48	40	-12

Ryan was selected 1st Round, 4th Overall by the Sarnia Sting in the 2011 OHL Priority Selection Draft from the Sudbury Wolves Minor Midget program. Ryan joined a very deep Sarnia Sting forward group as they were looking to make a big playoff run. He gained limited ice in Sarnia as a 16 year old but when the trade deadline approached he was dealt to the rebuilding Frontenacs where he received primarily 2nd line minutes. He also went on a nice statistical run showing what he's capable of.

This season was expected to be a huge coming out for the potential first rounder. However, Ryan really didn't play up to the expectations that were set out for him at the start of the season. When he's on he's a very dangerous offensive player. He displays very strong and creative passing ability. He can also make some good moves in one on one situations to beat defensemen and goaltenders. He has fairly quick hands and an effective shot. When he's on his game he engages very well along the boards and wins more than his share of battles.

The major issue with Kujawinski is his consistency. He has shown us these strengths in brief flashes, generally over a few shifts, then will disappear for long extents. He likely has the biggest combination of inconsistency and talent of any player entering the 2013 NHL Entry Draft. A consistent work ethic will be a huge improvement for Ryan and will likely be the difference of whether or not he makes it at the next level. We also need him to play more physical. Hits were generally few and far between in our viewings of Kujawinski. He's a tough player to gauge heading into this draft because he has shown glimpses of being a potential low end top six player, He will need to show this game in, game out, shift in, shift out, if he wants to reach his true potential which we believe, quite frankly, is higher than some of the players we see going ahead of him at the draft.

Quotable: "I found myself liking many of the 2014 eligible players on his team more than him during many of my viewings. Although in fairness to Ryan, that happened quite a bit this season around the OHL." – Mark Edwards

Brett Pesce

Defense -U of New Hampshire (NCAA)
Born Nov 15 1994 - Carrytown, NY
Height 6.02.75 - Weight 170 - Shoot R

Games	Goals	Assists	Points	PIMS	+/-
38	1	5	6	10	+6

Pesce is a steady defensive defenseman who limits the number of mistakes he commits with his solid positioning and good skating abilities. He will never be much of an offensive threat and will need to be very good in the defensive zone to make it to the pro level. He makes average first passes out of the zone, and possesses very limited playmaking abilities. His shot on the point definitely needs to improve, particularly getting them on net. Defensively, Pesce is a very solid presence. He is in good position time and time again, and makes it difficult for opponents to create good scoring chances. He has a very good stick that he uses to knock away passes, and is tough to play against along the walls. One area of improvement for Pesce would be his gap control. Despite his good skating ability, at times leaves too big of a gap off the rush. We expect that like many players, once he learns to trust his skating ability and be a little more aggressive, he will become an even more effective defenseman in the future.

Ryan Fitzgerald

Centre – Valley Jr. (EJHL)
Born Oct 19, 1994 – Boca Raton, FL
Height 5.09.5 - Weight 168 - Shoots R

Games	Goals	Assists	Points	PIMS	+/-
26	14	16	30	50	N/A

Despite his small stature, Fitzgerald oozes skill and hockey sense. He plays a smooth two-way game with great awareness of time, space, and pressure. He's a shifty skater with quick hands and is very deceptive with the puck, able to beat defenders 1-on-1 with swift changes of direction and outstanding skill. He plays with a lot of jump, keeps his feet moving and his head up, actively tracking the play. He is apt at finishing plays as he can pick spots with quick shots. His penalty killing is solid and he covers well in his own zone. He shows an active stick in all three zones. His size is an issue at times, as bigger players can overpower him. He generally shows good evasiveness but when keyed in on by the opposing team, he can have a tough time making an impact. He is guilty of trying to do too much at times, which though not a major issue at the EJHL level due to his ability to quickly cover his mistakes with strong back checking could become a concern as he progresses. Ryan is committed to Boston College and is expected to start this fall of 2013.

Gustav Olofsson

Defense - Green Bay Gamblers (USHL)
Born Dec 1, 1994 – Boras, Sweden
Height 6.02.75 - Weight 185 - Shoot L

HOCKEYPROSPECT.COM

DRAFT GUIDE' 13

Games	Goals	Assists	Points	PIMS	+/-
63	2	21	23	59	+11

Gustav is a Swedish-born, mostly US-raised blueliner who plays a strong all-around game and will suit up for Colorado College in the fall. He takes care of his end first and foremost by making himself hard to play against with strong stick and body checking against the rush, along the boards, and in front of his net. His positioning is sound and he's strong on his feet. He has an affinity for contact, and as such goes for big hits from time to time. He usually picks his spots well but does sometimes take himself out of the play. He shows good offensive upside with a smart first pass and intelligent reads with the puck in his end. At times, he rushes the puck with poise and can be useful on the power play with smart point play, but his puck skills have yet to manifest on a consistent basis. His point shot in particular needs to be refined as he has a hard time getting it on net. He's a safe pick based on his defensive play and considering his lanky frame and developing offensive game, he has the potential to round out into a solid NHL blueliner.

Philippe Desrosiers

Goalie – Rimouski Oceanic (QMJHL)
Born Aug 16, 1995 – St. Hyacinthe, QC
Height 6.01.25 - Weight 182 - Catch L

HOCKEYPROSPECT.COM

DRAFT GUIDE' 13

Games	Wins	Losses	G.A.A	Save %	SO
43	22	8	3.07	0.900	1

Philippe plays a standard butterfly style with tremendous attention to details and accurate positioning. He is calm and compacted in his crease. He plays the angles and positional game like very few 17 years old goalie do. He doesn't display much excess movement and doesn't get ahead of the play allowing him to maintain ideal positioning in his crease. This great positioning helps him tremendously in regards to rebound control consistently absorbing pucks and he pushes other shots into corners well. He handles the puck fairly well and likes to go out of his net to play the puck and initiating the transition himself. His reads are great and his anticipation is a very strong quality in Desrosiers' game. These attributes help him again move laterally at the right moments to get in great position. Desrosiers has good reflexes, but still need to improve his glove. His mental toughness is great, performing well at the most important times and quickly forgetting a bad goal he allowed. He has consistency that teams will look for, rarely stealing a game on his own but as well, rarely having a terrible game.

Nick Sorensen

RW – Quebec Remparts (QMJHL)
Born Oct 23, 1994 – Holback, DEN
Height 6.00.75 - Weight 166 - Shoot L

Games	Goals	Assists	Points	PIMS	+/-
46	20	27	47	18	+10

Nick is a great skater, possessing a tremendous explosiveness making him dangerous when he has the puck crashing the net. A dynamic skater that is tough to stop when he handles the puck at his top speed. He is a very good finisher and finds countless ways to put the puck in the back of the net. He is not afraid of high traffic areas, being able to position his stick at the right place and doing the little details that a good goal scorer can. His wrist shot is released quickly with great accuracy. He makes good, quick decisions showing high hockey IQ. He is not a selfish player and will use his good passing skills to create a scoring chance for a teammate. Sorensen's defensive instincts are solid which makes him a good two-way player when he's focused in the game. He still needs to get bigger and stronger to win battles along the boards, but his progression throughout the year in this particular area is undeniable. He seems to be able to elevate his play in the crucial moments of the game. He does have a bad tendency to rely on his skill lacking a consistent work ethic.

Wilhelm Westlund

Defense – Farjestad Jr. (SWE-JR)
Born Mar 15, 1995 – Stockholm, SWE
Height 5.11.25 - Weight 184 - Shoot L

Games	Goals	Assists	Points	PIMS	+/-
33	3	12	15	76	+10

He has games where he plays excellent hockey, but Westlund is in many ways still trying to put it all together. At his best, he plays mistake free hockey. He made the jump to the Elitserien this year and has not looked out of place, keeping it simple in generally limited ice time. He shows a good active stick, especially against the rush, and keeps his head on a swivel at all times. His skating is strong, with good agility and first step quickness. He shows a lot of poise for his age, evading the forecheck and making a solid first pass. With Sweden at U18 tournaments this year, he showed offensive upside with puck-rushing ability and a good selection of shots. At times, sometimes for whole games, his defensive coverage is off a step. He can have trouble with speed to the outside and can be too tentative. He could stand to play more physically in his end, but is limited in part by his size. He lacks elite upside, but has played well against men this year and projects as a strong two-way player.

Eric Comrie

Goalie – Tri-City Americans (WHL)
Born July 6, 1995 – Edmonton, AB
Height 6.00.75 - Weight 174 – Catch L

HOCKEYPROSPECT.COM DRAFT GUIDE '13

Games	Wins	Losses	G.A.A	Save %	SO
37	20	14	2.62	0.915	2

His game has been rock solid and it is rare to see such a young player play such a composed game. The technical game of Comrie is quite solid. He has a good, wide butterfly and is very quick on his knees to go post to post. He has the ability to quick recover after giving up a rebound and making a huge save because of his quickness. He tracks pucks through traffic effectively. Comrie plays with such poise and traffic out front doesn't affect him. He also seems to have a short memory as he does not let bad goals affect him either. A great example is the number of times that he got pulled this season. Out of 37 starts, he was only pulled once against a lethal Portland team. An area of improvement for Comrie would be his puck handling abilities. His puck playing is limited to none as he is not good at the basic things like stopping the puck for his defensemen behind the net let alone passing the puck up ice or clearing it. It will be interesting if Comrie's athleticism has regressed due to his hip surgery.

Niklas Hansson

Defense – Rogle Jr. (SWE-JR)
Born Jan 8 1995– Helsingborg, SWE
Height 6.00.5 - Weight 175 - Shoots R

HOCKEYPROSPECT.COM DRAFT GUIDE '13

Games	Goals	Assists	Points	PIMS	+/-
39	3	20	23	47	-16

Niklas is a two-way defenseman who lacks polish but has plenty of upside. He's strong offensively. His outlet passes are excellent, whether long bombs or short, safe dishes. He plays the point well on the power play with good keeps and a hard one-timer, though he could stand to improve his accuracy as he frequently misses the target. He can skate the puck with poise when given room and stickhandles well, but his skating lacks explosiveness, which makes it difficult for him to beat defenders outright. In his own zone, his unrefined footwork can cause him problems tracking the cycle, with slow starts and stops, and evading the forecheck when picking up a loose puck. His coverage is generally good, with particularly strong positioning against the rush where he angles off effectively and finishes his checks well. He's not the most physical player but he plays the body capably. Bigger forwards give him trouble, especially in front of his net. He still has a lot of room to add onto his frame, which will not only improve his strength but should also boost his confidence and in turn improve all aspects of his game.

Jonathan Diaby

Defense - Victoriaville Tigres (QMJHL)
Born Nov 16, 1994 – Montreal, QC
Height 6.05 - Weight 223 - Shoots L

Games	Goals	Assists	Points	PIMS	+/-
67	4	22	26	117	+12

What caught our eye first about Diaby is his ability to play in a 1-on-1 situation. His improved mobility allows him to react well and make an excellent use of his body and stick to stop his opponents. A prime example was in a game against the Halifax Mooseheads when he spent all night defending Nathan Mackinnon and Jonathan Drouin. Diaby was a step-ahead of them the entire time and did a great job defending them. He also displays impressive strength along the board and in front of the net. He has also displayed his toughness dropping the gloves. However this side of the game disappeared as he became a more critical member of his team in all game situations. His play with the puck has always been an issue for us since he entered the league, but it has improved drastically this year. He now plays safely with the puck from his own end and can execute a solid transition most of the time. The main component missing from his game that prevents us from ranking him higher is his hockey sense at times.

Juuse Saros

Goaltender – HPK (SM-liiga)
Born April 19, 1994 – Forssa, Finland
Height 5.10 - Weight 180 – Catches L

Games	Wins	Losses	G.A.A	Save %	SO
37	N/A	N/A	1.86	0.933	4

Saros has moved up the ranks with HPK rather rapidly and started in goal as a 16 year old in the U20 league posting very good numbers last season. He returned to this league and showed his talents internationally as well. Juuse will need to overcome his size. It's what's made us most cautious about him as 5'10" is a tough height to succeed at the NHL level as a goaltender. However, Juuse seems to be defying the odds at this point of his development. Hands down his best attribute is his leg movement. It looks like someone hit the turbo button every time he drops into the butterfly. What's more impressive is how quickly he gets up. His leg movement is simply outstanding and when you mix it with his vision through traffic and technical abilities it makes him a very talented goaltender. He has excellent reflexes and his glove hand is great. He also has great recovery and looks poised when making multiple saves in succession. He has trouble with rebound control and will need to improve this. He's quick enough to make the save, but it will be more of a concern at a higher level. Juuse is a good puck playing goaltender and doesn't rush or panic making intelligent passes up ice or clearing the zone.

Greg Betzold

Left Wing - Peterborough Petes (OHL)
Born March 11, 1995 – Bel Air, MD
Height 6.01.5 - Weight 195 - Shoots L

HOCKEYPROSPECT.COM DRAFT GUIDE' 13

Games	Goals	Assists	Points	PIMS	+/-
67	9	23	32	32	-11

Greg signed with the Petes as a free agent and became a valuable contributor for them all season. Greg often plays a pro style game and is at his best when he sticks to it. He works hard and wins tons of puck battles. He cycles the puck well and does a good job getting the puck to the scoring areas. While he did not have many goals this season, we believe they are going to come. His best skill is his ability to control the puck, beat defenseman and then use his creativity to create scoring chances. Besides his offensive abilities, Greg displayed a fantastic work ethic all season. He came into the OHL raw, and by the end of the season was a strong three zone player, and consistently one of the hardest workers on the ice. Greg could stand to finish more of his checks. He had games where this was a strength and others where he left hits on the ice. We would like to see him trust his possession skills a little more. Overall, we see Betzold as a player with tremendous upside. With added strength, and improved skating over the summer, Greg appears set to be a big part of the Petes' next season in the OHL.

Spencer Martin

Goalie – Mississauga Steelheads (OHL)
Born June 8, 1995 – Oakville, ON
Height 6.02.25 - Weight 198 – Catch L

HOCKEYPROSPECT.COM DRAFT GUIDE' 13

Games	Wins	Losses	GAA	Save%	SO
46	17	21	3.02	0.906	0

After being one of the top rated goaltenders to go into the 2011 OHL Priority Selection Draft, Spencer showed his abilities in limited opportunities, so much that Mississauga was comfortable trading away their long time veteran goaltender J.P. Anderson. Martin got off to a flying start this season and was a huge factor in his teams early success. He is am agile kid with good recovery skills. He does a pretty good job of making himself big and staying square to the shooter. He is very calm in the net and doesn't provide very much excess movement which allows him to consistently maintain strong positioning. His recovery skills are good although sometimes he seems to overplay a few shots when he goes across his net. Martin is technically sound and combines that with his great size.. A friend of mine coached him for two years leading up to his OHL draft selection. He raved about both Martin the goalie and the person.

Justin Bailey

Right Wing - Kitchener Rangers (OHL)
Born July 1, 1995 – Buffalo, NY
Height 6.03 - Weight 186 – Shoots R

HOCKEYPROSPECT.COM

DRAFT GUIDE' 13

Games	Goals	Assists	Points	PIMS	+/-
57	17	19	36	34	+22

Justin had a moderately successful rookie season in the OHL this yaer. Things started out slowly for Justin receiving ice primarily on the 4th line. He never really moved beyond the 3rd line this season due to the tremendous depth and veteran presence on the Rangers. Bailey's work ethic improved and he battled for loose pucks and attempted to create turnovers. Justin likes to have the puck on his stick and is always looking for scoring opportunities in the offensive zone. He has shown some flashes of creativity with the puck. He works hard to be reliable in the defensive zone and is good at assisting his defenders down low. He has a tremendous shot that fools many goaltenders. His skating stride is fairly choppy and he has issues generating speed in his first few steps. Although he is capable of reaching a good speed for a 6'3" forward. Bailey has size but rarely gets involved in the physical aspect of the game, which may be a confidence issue at this point. He should look to add strength to his frame in the offseason in preparation for next year.

William Carrier

LW - Cape Breton Screaming Eagles (QMJHL)
Born Dec 20, 1994 – La Salle, QC
Height 6.01.5 - Weight 198 - Shoots L

HOCKEYPROSPECT.COM

DRAFT GUIDE' 13

Games	Goals	Assists	Points	PIMS	+/-
34	16	26	42	41	-14

Carrier has a great mix of skating, skills, power and goal scoring abilities. He makes all of these abilities look effortless. His puck protection is one of the best in the QMJHL. He has a great variety of accurate shots that he can release quickly. Combined with a superb forehand-to-backhand move is also key to Carrier's success. He handles the puck well in traffic and his large frame also gives him an extra second to make his play on the boards. An underrated passer, William sees the ice well and can execute some intricate plays on the rush and when he controls the play on the powerplay. Carrier's biggest weakness and what has been worrying us all year in our viewings is the lack of effort and passion he displays on the ice. In his own zone, he rarely moved his feet and showed a satisfying compete level. We didn't see a game of William Carrier this year where he showed consistency in his effort. Defensively, Carrier still has a lot to learn, focusing, making the necessary sacrifices and keeping his position better. He also made too many costly turnovers. He has a lot of upside but has a very long way to go before we start seeing William reach his potential.

Jordan Subban

Defence – Belleville Bulls (OHL)
Born Mar 3, 1995 - Toronto, ON
Height 5.09 - Weight 175 - Shoots R

HOCKEYPROSPECT.COM

DRAFT GUIDE '13

Games	Goals	Assists	Points	PIMS	+/-
68	15	36	51	47	+22

Jordan's style of game resembles that of his older brother P.K. Subban. A smooth skating, puck rushing defenseman who likes to jump in on the attack and provide the team with offense from the back end. He is agile with good moves to get around defenders or create space to work with from the opposition and reads the play well to step off the point and come down into the high slot to put good shots on net. He makes a great first pass out of the zone to start the rush and gets his shots through to the net from the point kept down low to try to generate rebounds. Jordan also provides a gritty agitating style of game and has a great ability to get under the skin of his opposition and throw them off their game. He needs to watch some of the turnovers trying to force passes through the opposition and is also a bit soft on the puck at times, getting knocked off it too easily. He also gives up a bit too much space sometimes in his own end, leaving the opposition with the opportunity to get a pretty good shot off with time and space.

Keaton Thompson

Defense – USNTDP (USHL)
Born Sep 14, 1995 - Edina, MN
Height 6.00.25 - Weight 187 - Shoot L

HOCKEYPROSPECT.COM

DRAFT GUIDE '13

Games	Goals	Assists	Points	PIMS	+/-
57	4	14	18	38	-2

Keaton is a tough player to accurately project. Some days he looks like a first rounder, others he makes us check the line-up sheet to make sure he's on the ice. He's an excellent skater and when he's on his game, his decision-making is near perfect. He's not overly physical, but intelligent, aware, poised, and fundamentally sound, with pinches at the right times, puck-rushing ability, excellent passing, the ability to quarterback a power play and get pucks on net, and instinctive and smooth defensive zone positioning. Unfortunately, he hasn't shown that he can play at his peak on a consistent basis. Far from it. Most games, Thompson frustrates with consistently bad reads and giveaways. The tools are still there, but the decision-making is lacking. Thompson played his best hockey in early season viewings and by the end of the campaign, was having a rough go of it just about every single night. A poor showing at the U18 World Junior Championships in Sochi put a disappointing cap on his season.

Teemu Kivihalme

Defense – Burnsville (HIGH-MN)
Born Mar 9, 1995 - Duluth, MN
Height 5.11.25 - Weight 161 - Shoot L

HOCKEYPROSPECT.COM

DRAFT GUIDE' 13

Games	Goals	Assists	Points	PIMS	+/-
25	9	21	30	22	+1

Teemu's game revolves around excellent skating, which he uses to maneuver swiftly around the ice with and without the puck. He's a smooth stickhandler with excellent offensive upside, able to rush the puck end-to-end with poise. He excels at running an offense from the point, especially on the powerplay, where he uses quick footwork and good puck skills to make plays. He frequently looks to jump into the attack and is responsible about dropping back when he should. His defensive zone play needs some refining. He sometimes lacks urgency with the puck in his end. He shows an active stick but his positioning can be off by a step or two, especially against the rush where his gap control is inconsistent and although he's improved in this area, he can still be overly aggressive at times. He's not physically involved enough on the boards and in front of the net, though shows an edge from time to time. Adding bulk will really help improve his game, as he's still very lean and lanky. His tools are excellent, but he's still raw.

Juuso Ikonen

Left Wing – Blues (SM-liiga)
January 3, 1995 – Espoo, FIN
Height 5.09 - Weight 169 - Shoots L

HOCKEYPROSPECT.COM

DRAFT GUIDE' 13

Games	Goals	Assists	Points	PIMS	+/-
57	13	13	26	4	+1

Ikonen is an undersized Finnish winger who possesses a good skating ability and is generally pretty strong on his feet for a smaller player. He is fairly easy to move off the puck but almost always stays on his feet although bigger opponents win majority of puck battles along the boards. Jusso is good at making smart passes and moves the puck effectively up the ice although he sometimes has a habit of trying to be too fancy which can sometimes result in turnovers. He needs to improve his positioning and awareness in the defensive zone as he sometimes is caught standing around or flying the zone too early before the puck is in total possession.

Brian Pinho

Center – St. John's Prep (HIGH-MA)
Born May 11, 1995 – Beverly, MA
Height 6.00 - Weight 173 - Shoots R

HOCKEYPROSPECT.COM DRAFT GUIDE '13

Games	Goals	Assists	Points	PIMS	+/-
21	12	24	36	24	N/A

The smooth, dynamic Pinho plays a strong two-way game and was head and shoulders above his competition playing high school hockey in Massachusetts this year. He is an absolute force with the puck, acting as quarterback at even strength and on the power play with the skill to take over on every shift. His skating is fluid and precise with great acceleration. He buys time and space with elite stick handling in the neutral and offensive zones, and uses his reach and frame well. He can play the point on the power play and shows off an excellent wrist shot, snapshot, and one-timer. Pinho could stand to distribute better but is likely acting on coach's orders with St. John's as his finishing ability is strong enough that he can threaten even when keyed on by opponents. He forechecks and back checks intelligently, using an active stick more than his body to capably strip the puck and force mistakes. He battles hard for rebounds and positioning in front of the net and wins pucks along the boards with quick stick work. Best of all, he's still lanky with room to add muscle to his frame.

Bogdan Yakimov

Centre – Nizhnekamsk 2 (VHL)
Born Oct. 4, 1994 – Nizhnekamsk, RU
Height 6.05 - Weight 202 - Shoots L

HOCKEYPROSPECT.COM DRAFT GUIDE '13

Games	Goals	Assists	Points	PIMS	+/-
11	6	7	13	2	+6

Yakimov spent all of last season, and the first part of this season with Reaktor Nizhnekamsk of the MHL. During that time he also played for Team Russia at the 2011 and 2012 IIHF World U18 Championships. After opening this season in the MHL, he split the remainder of the season with Dizel Penza and Izhstal Izhevsk both of the VHL. The first thing you notice about Bogdan Yakimov is his size. He's a big forward with a huge frame and he protects the puck well. Despite lacking skating ability he has the hands to evade defensemen in one on one situations, but likely won't be able to do that against defensemen at higher levels. Yakimov shows no hesitation using his size to battle for pucks but unfortunately loses far too many battles for someone his size. He needs to get better in these battles because he gets right in there and fights for pucks in all three zones. Skating is the biggest area of improvement. He struggles getting up and down the ice and will likely be what drops him out of the spot his size and puck skills could have him. He has a very hard shot and seems to be his go to offensive weapon as he shoots a lot more than passes.

John Hayden

Center - USNTDP (USHL)
Born Feb 14, 1995 – Chicago, IL, USA
Height 6.02.5 - Weight 210 - Shoots R

HOCKEYPROSPECT.COM

Games	Goals	Assists	Points	PIMS	+/-
45	15	14	29	74	+13

John is a tough, two-way forward who is nasty to play against. His fore checking ability is excellent with good timing and great hitting, and he has shown relentless willingness to battle and force turnovers. He also back checks hard, plays the body in the neutral and defensive zones, and is strong on the penalty kill. Although there isn't much fighting in the USHL, John dropped the gloves a few items during the season and at the USHL Top Prospects Game and will defend his teammates when necessary. He brings the same type of energy offensively, but lacks touch. He's at his most effective in the dirty areas but when it comes to finishing plays, hitting open teammates with passes, and carrying the puck through the neutral zone, he's inconsistent. He can bulldoze the puck to the net from behind or the corners and can screen the goaltender, so he can be useful even without finesse. He's a safe bet to be an effective professional in a bottom-six role, and could eventually slot into a top-six role with the right line mates but realistically his offensive upside is limited.

Sven Andrighetto

Right Wing - Rouyn-Noranda (QMJHL)
Born Mar 21, 1993 – Zurich, SUI
Height 5.10 - Weight 180 - Shoots L

HOCKEYPROSPECT.COM

Games	Goals	Assists	Points	PIMS	+/-
53	31	67	98	45	+25

Andrighetto possesses elite offensive tools and is one of the most talented players in the QMJHL. His skating abilities are great, whether it's his rarely matched top speed, superb acceleration or his fantastic agility. His puck-control is amazing and it seems like the puck is glued to his stick. He will get past defenders by using speed instead of trying to go through the players with a slick move which is something we really like to see. He possesses a rocket of a shot, with a lethal release on his wrist shot or his slapshot. Andrighetto has improved his defensive game a lot in the past season, showing more maturity his position and in the way he will rarely cheat or skip a backcheck to take a chance offensively. He is willing to battle on the boards to retrieve the puck and is not afraid of getting hit. He's not a big player and will need to bulk up to be as effective in pro hockey, but has proven that he can physical abuse and keep the puck against bigger players on multiple occasions. We like the character he has, being able to produce and make big plays for his team offensively and defensively.

Anthony Duclair

Left Wing – Quebec Remparts (QMJHL)
Born Aug 26, 1995 - Pointe-Claire, QC,
Height 5.11 - Weight 177 - Shoots L

HOCKEYPROSPECT.COM

DRAFT GUIDE'13

Games	Goals	Assists	Points	PIMS	+/-
55	20	30	50	22	+23

Anthony Duclair is a tremendous skater blessed with amazing explosiveness. He has quick hands and can control the puck quite well at top speed. Although we feel he can still improve his finish, Anthony Duclair generates plenty of scoring chances for himself and could have doubled his number of goals scored with better opportunism. He's an underrated passer, setting up many plays with crisp and accurate passes. speed he has in his skating and execution, he dominated as a forward when he played this way. His worst moments were when he played a soft peripheral game, choosing to rely on skills and East-West play. He subsequently appeared overconfident, gliding and not especially focused in the decisions he was making with the puck. He has to show better consistency in the way he plays and the intensity he brings each night. He's not the type of player that will go out of his way to block a shot and further, we would like to see the same kind of speed he uses offensively put to use defensively.

Jeff Corbett

Defenseman – Sudbury Wolves (OHL)
Born Sept 20, 1994 – Uxbridge, ON
Height 6.01.5 - Weight 170 - Shoots L

HOCKEYPROSPECT.COM

DRAFT GUIDE'13

Games	Goals	Assists	Points	PIMS	+/-
45	3	10	13	36	+9

Jeff came on to our radar later on in the season and we like what we saw. Played some smart minutes and didn't show any big gaps in his game. He played smart and moved the puck effectively. Seemed to get better as the game progressed. Skating was solid and he showed good feet.

Quotable: "Maybe a little raw at this point of his development, but I see some potential in his game." - Mark Edwards

Connor Clifton

Defense – USNTDP (USHL)
Born April 28, 1995 - Long Branch, NJ
Height 5.10.75 - Weight 175 - Shoot R

HOCKEYPROSPECT.COM

DRAFT GUIDE' 13

Games	Goals	Assists	Points	PIMS	+/-
56	7	11	18	122	+11

Clifton isn't the biggest kid but he's physically strong and keeps other teams honest with his physicality. He's also diligent about clearing the front of his net and playing heavy on the boards. He's a hard worker and rarely takes a shift off. Clifton's game is tied together with excellent skating. He accelerates quickly and is very strong on his feet, allowing him to fight off checks. Clifton's offensive game is evolving. He shows flashes of dynamic puck-rushing ability and can go end-to-end with poise and determination. He likes to join the rush and pinch into the attack and, for the most part, does so without being a liability. He has a good shot though his accuracy is inconsistent. The biggest question here is discipline. Clifton can be overzealous in his pursuit of contact and sometimes crosses the line although he has gotten a little better over the course of the season. He has the tools to progress into an excellent defenseman. It's fair to predict that he'll continue to refine his game. There's a lot of upside here for a team willing to be patient.

Rushan Rafikov

Defense – Yaroslavl 2 (MHL)
Born May 15, 1995 – Saratov, RUS
Height 6.02 - Weight 181 - Shoots L

HOCKEYPROSPECT.COM

DRAFT GUIDE' 13

Games	Goals	Assists	Points	PIMS	+/-
53	1	9	10	38	+11

Rushan is a throwback defender. He plays a strong defensive game with a wicked edge. For forwards trying to come into his corner or camp out in front of the net, he makes life hell with gritty stick work and hard hits. He's difficult to beat wide and steps up at the blueline when he sees the opportunity. He relishes contact and likes to mix it up after the whistles, though he can overdo it and at times takes ill-advised penalties.

His offensive game is limited. He makes a good first pass and has a nice point shot, but lacks real upside with the puck. He pinches decisively and physically, leading with the stick and making heavy contact on 50/50 pucks. He's a good leader and takes few shifts off.

Gustav Possler

Right Wing – MODO JR. (SWE-JR)
Born Nov 11, 1994 - Sodertalje, SWE
Height 6.00 - Weight 183 - Shoots L

HOCKEYPROSPECT.COM DRAFT GUIDE '13

Games	Goals	Assists	Points	PIMS	+/-
36	19	21	40	28	+14

Gustav has a real nose for the net, and is consistently a threat to score from the slot. The first thing you notice about Possler's game is his offensive abilities. He is very quick off the rush and shows good poise with the puck. He has above average stick handling abilities and while he may not overwhelm any defender with his hands, he is able to protect the puck and control it effectively with speed. Possler's best asset is his shooting ability. He has a very good release to his shots, and is also able to place them quite accurately. He is not afraid to crash the net, and show some toughness and be willing to mix it up with opposing defensemen. The weakness to Possler's game is his defensive abilities. There are times when he floats around the ice without the puck, and will need to really improve on playing with more intensity in his own end. He certainly has the offensive tools to be a successful pro, but if he cannot be trusted by his coaches in the defensive zone, he will not have the opportunity to show off his skills in the offensive zone.

Anton Cederholm

Defense – Rogle Jr. (SWE-JR)
Born Feb 21, 1995 – Helsingborg, SW
Height 6.01.5 - Weight 204 - Shoots L

HOCKEYPROSPECT.COM DRAFT GUIDE '13

Games	Goals	Assists	Points	PIMS	+/-
36	5	8	13	64	+34

Anton has worked his way up the Rogle system playing U16, J18 and J20 games as a 15 year old and didn't look back playing in the J20 since with the exception of a few games here and there. He worked his way up to the Elitserien this season playing 12 games in the men's league. Unfortunately Rogle was relegated to the Allsvenskan league for the 2013-2014 season. Anton is a big bodied defenseman who loves to play physical and use his size to intimidate his opponents. He makes some huge open ice hits and destroys opponents along the boards. In one on one situations he utilizes both his stick and his body to make good plays and is reliable defensively. Anton moves the puck incredibly well and shows the ability to create breakout situations moving the puck over two lines and hitting his man tape to tape. He moves the puck intelligently in all three zones, but generally doesn't do much more offensively other than move the puck well. He needs to work on his skating ability but it's not a major concern at this point. He will never put up a ton of offensive points but he plays a solid, mean, physical defensive game and chips in with his smart puck moving ability.

Joose Antonen

Wing – JYP 2 (Finland-2)
Born April 28, 1994 – Tampere, FIN
Height 6.01.5 - Weight 204 - Shoots R

Games	Goals	Assists	Points	PIMS	+/-
30	5	6	11	20	+0

Joose is talented, but enigmatic. He has the size and skill to play an excellent power game. He can bring the puck down the wing with great speed and protection, and flashes talent with deft stick handling, quality passes through sticks and bodies, and an excellent wrist shot. He is smart with the puck along the boards and can shield defenders off well. However, the effort level is not always there. Often, he looks sluggish on the ice with labored movement, whiffed shots, and at times neglects to put in any kind of back checking or fore checking effort. Even when he gets his shots off, his accuracy is questionable. His attention to detail is sorely lacking. He teases with shifts where he turns it on and looks like a prospect, but doesn't consistently show a strong enough compete level.

Yan-Pavel Laplante

Center – PEI Rocket (QMJHL)
Born April 23, 1995 – Amqui, PQ
Height 6.00 - Weight 178 - Shoots L

Games	Goals	Assists	Points	PIMS	+/-
18	5	8	13	12	+11

Laplante injured his shoulder seriously at the Ivan Hlinka Under-18 tournament in August and had to wait until February to play his first game of the season. He came back in top shape and impressed us in our viewings with both the PEI Rockets and at the IIHF World Under-18 Championship. Laplante is a gifted puck handler with great speed and goal scoring instincts. He has quick hands and could dangle in a phone booth. He gets in a scoring position when he doesn't have the puck, whether he is in the high slot or crashing the net for a chance to jump on a rebound. He can execute some high quality passing plays, but will always prefer the shot. This season he put more effort defensively consistently moving his feet. He showed the will to block shots and back check hard. He still needs to improve his consistency as he tends to wait for the important moments before doing those little details. He can be selfish at times, hanging on to the puck for too long forcing shots. We feel Laplante made the most out of his limited games played this season.

Hudson Fasching

Right Wing – USNTDP (USHL)
Born July 28, 1995 - Milwaukee, WI
Height 6.01.75 - Weight 213 - Shoot R

Games	Goals	Assists	Points	PIMS	+/-
56	10	17	27	39	+0

Hudson has seen his stock plummet since this time last year, and rightly so. He teases with great size and great flashes of offensive talent, but his hockey sense is questionable and infrequent. When he's on his game he moves well for his size, controls the puck well, shows good hands along the boards, and plays an intelligent, physical defensive game. More often than not, he has a hard time handling the puck and tries to force plays, leading to frustration and the rest of his game falling apart. It's easy to tell what kind of game Fasching will have based on his first shift. Part of his issues this year seemed to draw from puck luck as well, as he went stretches where he was ridiculously snake bitten with frequent goalposts and near misses. He also dealt with a concussion at the beginning of the season, and it's possible that the lingering effects of that were also a factor. Such negatives have a way of snowballing. Fasching will surely be drafted and will be looking at next year as a clean slate, which could help him get his game back together.

Zachary Sanford

Left Wing – Islanders (EJHL)
Born Nov 9, 1994 - Salem, MA
Height 6.03 - Weight 185 – Shoots L

Games	Goals	Assists	Points	PIMS	+/-
37	12	24	36	22	N/A

Perhaps no 2013 NHL Draft prospect has seen his stock rise this season like Sanford. At the onset of the season, he showed physical tools and played a gritty game in bursts, but showed slow feet and had a hard time handling the puck and working together with his teammates. Months later, he's a completely different player. Sanford shows ever-improving poise with the puck and has learned to better utilize his hands, which are deceptively quick for his size. He's strong on his stick and skates, allowing him to protect the puck well on the boards, though he can expose the puck with poor positioning at times. He makes plays in the offensive zone with intelligent passing, and can take the puck to the net with great force. He forechecks well with good contact and an active stick. His skating needs further improvement, as he's still choppy on his feet. He plays his best when he keeps things simple and focuses on going north-south, rather than trying to create. The Boston College-commit is still very raw, but shows flashes of being a dominant player.

Vincent Dunn

Center – Val d'Or Foreurs (QMJHL)
Born Sept 14, 1995 - Hull, QC, CAN
Height 5.11 - Weight 172 - Shoots L

HOCKEYPROSPECT.COM

DRAFT GUIDE'13

Games	Goals	Assists	Points	PIMS	+/-
53	25	27	52	98	+21

Dunn displays a great level of energy when he is on the ice which makes him very noticeable, rarely taking a shift off. He will try to get under the skin of his opponents, bantering after whistles, starting scrums, giving a little more on the body check and just knocking them off their game. Although he is not the biggest player Dunn will rarely refuse a fight and he has proven his willingness to drop the gloves. He is a tough player to play against because of his level of competitiveness. He doesn't necessary lay out the big hit often, but will be physical on the forecheck with high energy. He has an above-average top speed and great power in his first few strides to quickly reach max speed. He has quick hands and shows flashes of a talented skill set generating scoring chances. He has good vision and will score goals around the net, or on the rush. Defensively, Dunn has never stopped progressing, working hard and supporting his defensemen well. Dunn can overreact and be undisciplined and needs to control his temper.

Atte Makinen

Defenseman – Tappara Jr. (FIN-JR)
Born May 17, 1995 – Tampere, FIN
Height 6.03 - Weight 206 - Shoots R

HOCKEYPROSPECT.COM

DRAFT GUIDE'13

Games	Goals	Assists	Points	PIMS	+/-
40	5	9	14	71	+10

Makinen has worked his way up the Tappara program through the U16, U18 and U20's. This year he played primarily with the U20's getting a brief experience in Finland's 2nd Men's league playing four games with LeKi. Makinen is a big physical defenseman who takes pleasure in punishing opponents. Atte has arguably one of the best combinations of size and the aggression to hit as often as possible you'll find in this draft. He is tough along the boards and wins a lot of battles. He is very strong in one on one situations and provides a good gap control and very rarely gets beaten. He can go through stretches where he's pretty quiet but that is a good thing for a defenseman who plays the type of game Makinen does. He isn't much of an offensive contributor but he has shown the ability to move the puck well and even a few flashes of puck rushing protecting the puck with his big frame when given space. He can however be susceptible to puck playing mistakes or mishandling it when pressured. What you see is what you get with Makinen. He's physical, reliable, but won't put up too much offensively.

Connor Crisp

Center – Erie Otters (OHL)
Born April 8, 1994 – Alliston, ON
Height 6.04 - Weight 225 - Shoots L

HOCKEYPROSPECT.COM DRAFT GUIDE '13

Games	Goals	Assists	Points	PIMS	+/-
63	22	14	36	139	-31

Connor battles extremely hard out front of the opposing net making life difficult for goaltenders and defenders due to his huge frame. He has pretty good hands in the goal area and finishes many of his goals using his frame and his hands to put the puck in the back of the net. He finishes his checks regularly and isn't afraid to drop the gloves. Connor's ability to read plays and make quick decisions seems to go underrated because of his size and physicality but he regularly makes smart plays with the puck, but will have the occasional miscue. He contributed defensively, and while he wasn't exceptional in this area of the game, he was usually reliable. Connor has a huge frame and has the strength that will get him through junior, and should even help him at the pro level, but his skating is simply not good enough. He doesn't have very good quickness, he looks heavy on his feet, and this is an area that may scare off some teams. It will take a great deal of work for him to get his skating up to par and likely will never be an asset.

Tyler Ganly

Defense-S.S. Marie Greyhounds (OHL)
Born March 22, 1995 - Milton, ON
Height 6.01 - Weight 201 - Shoots R

HOCKEYPROSPECT.COM DRAFT GUIDE '13

Games	Goals	Assists	Points	PIMS	+/-
62	0	17	17	64	+2

Tyler started the season keeping things simple and ensuring a complete defense first attitude. As the season progressed he began to show more of a willingness to contribute to the offensive rush and take more chances with the puck. He is a big strong defender and is good at getting physical in the corners and front of the net in the defensive zone. He has been one of the most effective defensemen eligible in the draft in one on one situations and rarely got beat. He is a hard worker and generally makes strong simple crisp breakout passes and moves the puck quickly when pressured. Ganly is effective on the penalty kill and has shown a willingness to block shots and do whatever it takes to get the puck out of the defensive zone. He has also shown a willingness to stand up for teammates and dropped the gloves on a number of occasions over the season. Tyler needs to work on improving his offensive shot and adding some strength to his frame in order to really be able to dominate physically down low.

Daniel Nikandrov

Center – Sarnia Sting (OHL)
Born February 3, 1995 -
Height 6.01.5 - Weight 191 - Shoots L

Games	Goals	Assists	Points	PIMS	+/-
61	7	19	26	10	-5

Daniel came into this season essentially as rookie after playing only 7 games last year putting up two points. Daniel's strongest asset is his defensive awareness. He competes hard in his own zone, maintains good positioning and gets his sticks in lanes. Daniel has likely spent plenty of post games with a few bags of ice as he's more than willing to block shots. Daniel was Sarnia's best penalty killing forward by a wide margin this season. Nikandrov also competes along the wall. This developed over the course of the season and will likely improve further with increased strength. Daniel isn't a flashy offensive player but he is creative with the puck. He has good vision, hands and is an excellent passer. Many of his assists have come from high difficult passes made into easy finishes in the offensive zone. The chemistry he developed with top 2014 NHL Draft prospect Nikolay Goldobin was exceptional this season. Daniel is one of the best defensive forwards available in this draft and projects to be a solid bottom six forward

Dominik Kubalik

Left Wing – Sudbury Wolves (OHL)
Born August 21, 1995 – Czech Rep.
Height 6.01 - Weight 181 - Shoots L

Games	Goals	Assists	Points	PIMS	+/-
67	17	17	34	25	-3

Dominik spent the 2010-2011 and 2011-2012 rising up the ranks of HC Plzen from the U16 program all the way up to the Men's Czech Extraliga, scoring his first pro goal as a 16 year old. Dominik protects the puck really well to get a good cycle going in the offensive zone and has excellent moves to beat defenders and create space for himself and teammates. He is willing to go to the net to try to tip the puck and will play physical and make the big hits. He battles well for the puck to come out of the corners with it and gets down in lanes displaying a great willingness to block shots. He moves the puck around really well in the offensive zone to find lanes to get the puck to teammates which create good chances, and can find teammates in the slot with good passes. He can also move the puck to the high slot pretty well off the rush and will drive the puck towards the net. He rushes the puck up the ice pretty effectively with good speed and opens up nicely in the slot to take passes and put one-timers on from good scoring positions. Dominik plays a power game in North America which makes him well suited for different scenarios at the NHL level. The move to the OHL turned out to be a very good one for Dominik because it allowed him to show he can play that style on the small ice.

Kyle Platzer

Center – London Knights (QMJHL)
Born Mar 4, 1995 – Waterloo, ON
Height 5.11 - Weight 175 - Shoots R

Games	Goals	Assists	Points	PIMS	+/-
65	5	17	22	15	+7

Kyle came to Knights camp in September and made an impression after spending last year with the Waterloo Siskins Jr. B. He showed great chemistry on the fourth line with his line-mates one of which was fellow 2013 Eligible Remi Elie. Kyle displayed a strong work ethic and he competes every single shift. He isn't the biggest guy but wins more than his share of battles due to his never quit attitude. He displays good hockey sense and makes intelligent plays and seems to never hurt his team with his decisions even when pressured. Kyle chips in defensively playing very responsibly and maintains strong positioning. Kyle has shown some very good offensive skills at both the Minor Midget and Jr. B level but has just been able to show flashes of it at the OHL level. Watching Platzer play for 4 years and grow as a player, we feel there is a good chance he will start to show some good offensive skill when he becomes a more critical player for the Knights.

Marc-Olivier Roy

Center – Blainville (QMJHL)
Born November 5, 1994 - Ste-Foy, QC
Height 6.00 - Weight 175 - Shoots R

Games	Goals	Assists	Points	PIMS	+/-
65	29	38	67	68	+12

Roy is a great skater with good agility which helps him change direction quickly. His explosion is powerful helping him create space and be the first man to a loose puck. Roy has a good work ethic and great anticipation. He can be a very effective two-way forward when he plays with aggressiveness and keeps moving his feet. He has a good quick-release shot and likes to set it up on the half wall on the power play. His puck handling at top speed is great and he can be elusive when he's coming in a one on one situation putting his quick hands to good use. He can execute plays offensively exceptionally well at very high speeds. He sees the ice well and has a high level of hockey sense. Roy needs to go in the tough areas of the ice more frequently as he will find more success there than staying out in the perimeter. We have seen some games where Roy needs to keep his level of intensity at a higher level as he is a better player when he keeps his game simpler and plays with more grit. He will also need to get stronger moving forward.

Lucas Wallmark

RW – Skelleftea Jr
Born September 5, 1995 - Umea, SWE
Height 6.00 - Weight 176 - Shoots L

HOCKEYPROSPECT.COM

Games	Goals	Assists	Points	PIMS	+/-
14	5	11	16	18	+12

After starting off the year with Skellefteå, Wallmark was loaned to Karlskrona down the stretch where he was a factor in helping them stave off relegation, at times playing in the team's top six in crucial games. He is an excellent playmaker with fantastic hands, able to create time and space for his teammates with deft stick handling along the boards. He reads coverage patterns and can find holes in defenses with well-timed pinpoint passes. He has a good shot but tends to look for a passing option first, and when he does put the puck on the net it's often looking to create chances off rebounds. He's good back checker and has a good understanding of his defensive zone responsibility. Where he's limited is with his skating. He's agile in the offensive zone with good starts and stops, but in open ice he's slow-footed and awkward, limiting his ability to carry the puck up ice, forecheck, and back check.

Erik Bradford

Center – Barrie Colts (OHL)
Born Oct 19, 1994– Orangeville, ON
Height 5.11 - Weight 178 - Shoots L

HOCKEYPROSPECT.COM

Games	Goals	Assists	Points	PIMS	+/-
68	18	15	33	46	+8

The Colts really benefited from Erik's smart two-way play in this year's playoffs. Bradford plays a hard-nosed game with great work ethic mixed with an element of skill. He puts great pressure on the puck carrier, especially on the fore-check, and makes sure to finish all his hits along the boards. He is willing to go to the dirty areas and battle for pucks getting many of his opportunities off loose pucks and rebounds. He provides his defensemen with good support in his own end, tying up the opposition in front of the net as well as going down to get in lanes and block shots. He can cycle the puck effectively, brings a decent net-front presence in the offensive zone and possesses pretty good speed and agility to distance himself from the opposition's pressure when he has the puck. He moves the puck around well to start the rush, and likes to drive it wide with good protection, then throw it to the front of the net to teammates driving down the middle. He opens up nicely down low to take passes, then put good shots on net and will drive the puck to the net to create chances in tight. What makes him such an intriguing prospect is his level of hockey sense and ability to read and understand the play so quickly.

Nicholas Paul

Left Wing –Brampton Battalion (OHL)
Born March 20, 1995 – Mississauga
Height 6.02 - Weight 202 - Shoots L

Games	Goals	Assists	Points	PIMS	+/-
66	12	16	28	21	+6

Nicholas was selected in the 5th round of the 2011 OHL Priority Selection Draft by the Brampton Battalion out of the Mississauga Senators Minor Midget program. After a year in Minor Midget/OJHL Nicholas went into the Battalion training camp this season and earned a spot on the roster. In early and especially mid-season viewings, you could always find Paul playing physical, and showing a nice pair of hands in front of the net. He was not a good skater but was always able to remain involved in the play. However, towards the end of the season, he seemed to hit a wall likely due to playing his first full season at this level of play. He became a little more perimeter oriented and he essentially got away from his strengths. He is a strong player, who has a good chance to hear his name called at the 2013 NHL Entry Draft. When he sticks to his strengths he's an extremely effective player who plays a power game. However he needs to use the next season as an opportunity to elevate his play and show his true potential.

Miles Liberati

Defense – London Knights (OHL)
Born June 11, 1995 – Pittsburgh, PA
Height 6.01 - Weight 174 - Shoots L

Games	Goals	Assists	Points	PIMS	+/-
42	3	6	9	25	+5

Miles made the Knights out of camp but has had to fight for every minute of ice time playing on a very deep team. Miles has shown good two-way potential in our viewings of him this season. He likes to jump up in the rush, which he is effective at but needs to be careful at times not to get caught too far up ice. He has a good accurate shot from the point and can get it through. He is also smart and patient with the puck in all three zones. In his own zone he makes intelligent passes and is able to usually minimize turnovers although he does have the occasional mental error. Miles battles very hard in his own zone and shows a very strong compete level. He wins battles and fights for every inch in the defensive zone. In terms of improvement, Miles is a well rounded player who doesn't do anything particularly great, but doesn't have a single area that is a glaring weakness. We'd like to see him get stronger, faster and a lot of his improvements are going to be made by playing a regular every day shift next season when some of the veterans move on. He shows good puck skills, good defensive work ethic and can play a very good two-way game. He has average size for a defenseman, but can handle the physical battles at this level.

Jeremy Grégoire

Center – Baie Comeau (QMJHL)
Born Sept 5, 1995 – Sherbrooke, QC
Height 6.00 - Weight 190 - Shoots L

HOCKEYPROSPECT.COM

DRAFT GUIDE '13

Games	Goals	Assists	Points	PIMS	+/-
62	19	13	32	100	-9

Jeremy Grégoire is all about work ethic and going to the dirty areas. Most of his offensive production comes from tenacity around the net whether those are quick passing plays, finding soft areas to release shots or banging away on rebounds until they cross the goal line. He is able to produce extra intensity in front of the net to be the man jumping on the rebounds and holding his body position against older players. A big strong player, Grégoire competes really hard and has natural goal scoring instincts. He creates scrums, pushing and shoving with his intensity, he likes to agitate and provoke his opponents. He has great character and is willing to block shots and skate hard on the backcheck. Grégoire's biggest weakness is his skating. His top speed is below average for major junior and his explosiveness will needs improvement. He is limited in what he can do on the ice because of poor speed. He also has a tough time drawing a line when getting under the skin of players letting his emotions get the best of him at times.

Eric Roy

Left Wing – Exeter H.S. (HIGH-MN)
Born Dec 13, 1992 – Whitehouse, NJ
Height 6.01 - Weight 180 – Shoots R

HOCKEYPROSPECT.COM

DRAFT GUIDE '13

Games	Goals	Assists	Points	PIMS	+/-
72	17	22	39	37	-32

Roy is a big, offensive defenseman who has very good puck skills. He is able to move the puck smoothly and quite efficiently from the backend to start the attack. Roy is featured as the power play quarterback, and has done an admirable job since last season. The biggest concern with Roy is his defensive game. He is often caught in the middle of nowhere, and does not provide very good coverage in his own end. Offensively, Roy is quite impressive with and without the puck. He handles the puck smoothly and has very good control of it. Time and time again he is able to make very tight spins to get away from a forecheck to get the rush going up the ice. He makes good, crisp passes to his forwards, and limits the turnovers he commits. Roy has a good shot from the point, but needs to work on getting it on net and to use it if he has an open lane to the net. Roy may not be particularly quick, but he is able to cover a lot of ground with his long strides. He is good in tight areas with the puck, but he is slow to react when on defense. Another concern with Roy is his lack of toughness. He is fairly easy to bump off the puck, and does not show much desire to stand up for teammates in physical situations.

Jan Kostalek

Defense – Rimouski (QMJHL)
Born February 17, 1995 - Prague, CZE
Height 6.00 - Weight 174 - Shoots R

HOCKEYPROSPECT.COM

Games	Goals	Assists	Points	PIMS	+/-
48	5	13	18	53	+17

Kostalek plays a smart game in all three zones with simple yet effective execution. His top speed is effective but will need to improve before going pro. His explosiveness is already pretty good using it to pressure the puck carrier. Even when he was matched against bigger and stronger opponents, he was able to keep them on the outside resulting from his footwork, speed and great angling with his body. His physical play never stopped developing this season, throwing the body with more consistency as the season went on. Using his speed and hockey sense, he can play a physical and aggressive game without making too many positional mistakes. Kostalek has character and intensity in his game, willing to pay the price to make a play. He will use the safe chip play on the boards if there are no safe options available. He has a good slapshot and we would like him utilize it more frequently. We would like to see Jan become more confident with the puck as he can panic too often when pressured and turn the puck over.

Gregory Chase

C/LW – Calgary Hitmen (WHL)
Born Jan 1, 1995 – Sherwood Park, AB
Height 6.00 - Weight 195 - Shoots R

HOCKEYPROSPECT.COM

Games	Goals	Assists	Points	PIMS	+/-
69	17	32	49	58	+11

Chase is a playmaking forward who is at his best when he is moving his feet and playing with an edge. He likes to get involved physically and be in the middle of scrums, but needs to control himself to not take undisciplined penalties. He has been able to positively contribute to the success of the team and has received valuable minutes throughout the year. Greg Chase's best attribute is his playmaking ability. He has very good vision in the offensive zone, and makes good accurate passes for his teammates to receive great scoring chances. He uses his good speed down the wing to try to create some separation from opposing defensemen. He is able to read opposing coverage well and take advantage of any holes. Chase is deceptively quick on the ice. He does not move with great explosiveness out on the ice, but he is able to get from one area to another in a hurry. He is always in a battle for loose pucks, and has shown good strength. One issue with Chase's game is his inconsistency. He could be an offensive force in one game, then completely disappear the next game. He needs to consistently make a difference to have a better chance of playing at higher levels.

Carter Verhaeghe

Center – Niagara Ice Dogs (OHL)
Born Aug 14, 1995 - Toronto, ON
Height 6.01 - Weight 181 - Shoots L

Games	Goals	Assists	Points	PIMS	+/-
67	18	26	44	22	-12

As a rookie Carter received limited ice with a very talented Niagara Ice Dogs team that would go on to win the 2012 OHL Eastern Conference Championship. This year Verhaeghe moved up the draft rankings late in this season and finished the regular season with 6 goals, 9 points in his final 6 games. He posted 44 points in 67 games this season. Carter then joined Team Canada at the IIHF World U-18 Championship putting up 4 assists in 7 games playing a defensive role and helping Canada to a Gold Medal. Carter has been noticeably strong in the defensive zone and has been able to be a penalty killing specialist for the Ice Dogs at times. His most glaring weakness at the moment is his skating, which is an awkward style to say the least. We do expect that he will hear his name announced at the 2013 NHL Entry Draft. He projects to be a forward that can help his team out at both ends. However his skating simply has to improve. He will likely be a project who requires a few more seasons in the OHL and even a few AHL seasons to reach his potential.

Tyler Bertuzzi

LW – Guelph Storm (OHL)
Born Febr 24, 1995 – Sudbury, ON
Height 6.00 - Weight 178 - Shoots L

Games	Goals	Assists	Points	PIMS	+/-
43	13	9	22	68	-2

Bertuzzi had an up and down season for the Storm. He was forced to miss a large number of games due to an upper body injury. The Storm are a different team with Tyler in the lineup as he is constantly setting the physical tone and firing up teammates with his aggressive style of play. He can generate a good amount of space when given room to skate north and south along the boards and shows flashes of offensive creativity in one on one situations. Bertuzzi is at his best when he is driving to the net and outworking opposing defenders battling for rebound opportunities. Tyler is built very solid and he is very effective at getting under the skin of the opposition and works hard to draw penalties in scrums after the whistle. On the other edge of that sword, however, he can sometimes let his emotions get the best of him and take penalties himself. He has limited offensive upside at the pro level and will get many of his points from driving the net and working hard. Bertuzzi also needs to learn when to reign in his game and not allow himself to get out of position constantly chasing hits.

Roberts Lipsbergs

LW – Seattle Thunderbirds (WHL)
Born July 29, 1994 - Latvia
Height 5.10 - Weight 176 - Shoots L

Games	Goals	Assists	Points	PIMS	+/-
64	30	28	58	24	-11

Lipsbergs speed is very noticeable as he uses it on the forecheck and try to retrieve pucks. He plays hard at all times, and is not afraid of taking hits to make a play. He was one of the hardest workers for Seattle this season, and it showed as he received more and more important ice time as the season went along. Lipsbergs has good skills with the puck. He possesses above average playmaking skills, especially off the half wall after winning a battle for the puck, he will quickly move it to an open teammate for a good chance. He also has an above average shot, but it is something that he could improve on. His goals seem to come around the net mostly as he likes to drive the net. Defensively, Lipsbergs picked up more ice time in his own zone as the season went along. He improved on his coverage of the point and was good at moving around in the defensive zone to cover for teammates and help out when necessary. He could be a better shot blocker and provide some more impact in his own end, but it is clear that he is an offense first type of player.

Taylor Cammarata

LW/C – Waterloo (USHL)
Born May 13, 1995 - Minneapolis, MN
Height 5.07 - Weight 156 - Shoots L

Games	Goals	Assists	Points	PIMS	+/-
59	38	55	93	49	+39

Taylor scored with great consistency, going two straight games without a point just once. His production is largely based on his unpredictability. With the puck, Cammarata is a wizard with elite stick handling and lateral movement. He can evade checks with fantastic precision in the neutral and offensive zones and is extremely difficult to pin down. He's aware of everything happening on the ice and has the ability to alter the tempo of the game with the puck on his stick, showing outstanding vision and puck control in the process. He is nearly unstoppable on the power play when he has room to work with and shows off excellent passing, a great variety of hard, accurate shots, and fantastic poise. However, even at the USHL level, his size is clearly a limiting factor. Now known league-wide, Cammarata faces tough coverage on a nightly basis and is forced to endure serious physical punishment. He takes hits well but cannot be expected to continue to absorb contact at the same right against professionals. He eludes many checks but continuing to improve that aspect of his game will be essential if he wants to be productive in the future, much less prevent serious injury on a game-by-game basis.

Jackson Houck

RW – Vancouver Giants (WHL)
Born: Feb 27, 1995 - North Vancouver
Height 6.00 - Weight 186 - Shoots R

DRAFT GUIDE' 13

Games	Goals	Assists	Points	PIMS	+/-
69	23	34	57	68	-16

Houck is a physical, hard-working forward who has been the go-to offensive player for the Giants this season but projects well as a bottom six NHL player one day. He is one of the hardest working player on the team, and is consistently praised for his work ethic by those around him. Offensively, Houck has had to do a little bit of everything for the Giants this season. Whenever he was responsible for providing net front presence, Houck often came up with goals and showed above average hands in tight and the ability to take a beating but hold his ground. He is good along the boards and comes away with pucks on a consistent basis. Houck has played a key role in his own end for the Giants. He is not afraid to block shots, and reads the play well without the puck. Houck is difficult to play against when he is on the forecheck and delivers some big hits. The biggest improvement he needs to make is his skating. He has average speed, and when he plays against opponents that are faster than him, he has a difficult time keeping up.

Mason Geertsen

Defense – Vancouver Giants(WHL)
Born April 19, 95 – Drayton Valley, AB
Height 6.03 - Weight 199 – Shoots L

DRAFT GUIDE' 13

Games	Goals	Assists	Points	PIMS	+/-
58	2	8	10	98	-26

Geertsen joined the Giants midway through the season following a trade from Edmonton, and it has really helped him develop into a good defenseman. He is tough to play against in the defensive zone. He has a mean streak to his game, and will physically punish opponents in the slot and along the boards. He is good at reading the play without the puck, but he still has some improvements to make particularly when his goalie gives up a rebound and he has a tough time tracking it and trying to tie up opponents. He has let a few passes go cross crease which also led to dangerous chances. On the rush, Geertsen is a bit of a hit or miss. He has a good reach that he uses well, but when elite offensive players come down his wing with speed, he has difficulty at times of keeping them to the outside and not getting danced around by them. A big change in Geertsen's playing time has come from receiving power play minutes with the Giants. He has received the opportunity to quarterback the power play, and has not looked great doing so. He makes good, simple passes, but he does not read the play too well and does not make the greatest decisions with the puck. He also does not have the speed or skating abilities to rush the puck himself.

87

Wiley Sherman

Defense – Hotchkiss School (HS USA)
Born May 24, 1995 - Greenwich, CT
Height 6.06 - Weight 196 - Shoots L

HOCKEYPROSPECT.COM DRAFT GUIDE '13

Games	Goals	Assists	Points	PIMS	+/-
66	30	23	53	12	NA

Wiley intrigues as a huge defenseman who's a great skater for his size. He moves swiftly with a smooth stride and good edges. His defensive game is sharp. He's a calming presence who uses his long stick well to cover lanes and can play nasty, clearing the front of his net and making life difficult for forwards trying to play the puck along the boards. He's very aware and at times looked a step ahead of everybody else on the ice. He has a good shot from the point and can make a safe first pass out of his zone, but lacks the puck skills to say he has serious offensive upside at the next level. He rarely makes mistakes with the puck, but rarely makes things happen either. He played for a poor Hotchkiss team this year, which made it difficult to judge him properly, but showed very well at showcases playing against other top prospects from New England. He showed too many good things this season to pass through this draft unselected.

Ben Harpur

Defense – Guelph Storm (OHL)
Born Jan 12, 1995 – Hamilton, ON
Height 6.06 - Weight 210 - Shoots L

HOCKEYPROSPECT.COM DRAFT GUIDE '13

Games	Goals	Assists	Points	PIMS	+/-
67	3	12	15	59	+14

Harpur is a big bodied presence on the blue line and is good at using his size to lean on smaller forwards and clear out the front of the net. He needs to work at bringing a consistent physical presence to his game and finish more checks when given the opportunity. He is a good skater despite being such a big guy and has adequate speed to jump into the offensive rush when available. However, he has struggled in one on one situations at times due to a late pivot. He is good at using his long stick to keep opponents to the outside and is effective at getting into passing lanes and intercepting passes. Harpur is sometimes caught standing around in the defensive zone and needs to consistently pressure opposing forwards rather than let the play come to him. Harpur is good at getting his shots on net through traffic but needs to work at walking the line to create better shooting lanes. He will need to become a better skater and play a more tenacious game at his size. He does a variety of things well but nothing that stands out as exceptional. Harpur is a player we see going outside the first few rounds and selected to become a reliable defensive defenseman at the next level. One that doesn't play huge minutes but can be relied upon in his own end, and to hopefully play a penalty killing role as well.

Kurt Etchegary

Center – Quebec Remparts (QMJHL)
Born Nov 12, 1994 - St. John's, NL
Height 5.11 - Weight 185 - Shoots L

HOCKEYPROSPECT.COM

DRAFT GUIDE' 13

Games	Goals	Assists	Points	PIMS	+/-
31	9	16	25	56	10

He plays a smart positional game as he is not the fastest skater and will look bad if he starts running around. He has showed a lot of character by dropping the gloves against bigger opponents throughout his career. He plays defensive situations with smarts, determination and dedication. Kurt possesses great passing skills as he sees the ice very well. He can pass through skates and sticks with ease, finding teammates in traffic. He likes to delay the play when he enters the offensive zone, put his head up and create plays with his passing skills. He also showed his great offensive vision on the powerplay at multiple times in our viewings, creating scoring chances with superb cross-ice feeds. He will get goals when he crashes the net but he doesn't have a really good shot or the skating abilities to get in the slot before the opponent's defensive coverage is on him. He's not a gifted t puck handler and doesn't have the best puck control, regardless, he can still create some nice plays to keep the puck in tight space areas.

Anthony Florentino

Defense – South Kent (HS USA)
Born January 30, 1995 – Boston, MA
Height 6.00 - Weight 209 - Shoots R

HOCKEYPROSPECT.COM

DRAFT GUIDE' 13

Games	Goals	Assists	Points	PIMS	+/-
62	21	32	53	68	NA

The stocky blueliner had a nice season for the Selects, playing physical, defensive-minded hockey on a nightly basis and flashing a little offensive ability in the process. He's not the most agile skater, but he moves well for his size and can carry the puck up ice while building speed like a freight train. His hands are quick enough to make some plays and he gets good shots on net from the point, though he probably won't be a big point producer at the next level. He'll be able to clear danger with safe outlets and occasionally lug the puck, but his bread and butter is hard-nosed, positional defensive coverage. He impresses with smart reads against the rush, maintaining an active stick and stepping up to play the body when he can. He's aggressive behind his net and protects his crease with intensity, though he can get so caught up with laying contact in his end that he loses focus on the play and floats out of position. His footwork is an issue at times, especially when he jumps into the attack and doesn't hustle back to his end. He's strong enough positionally that his skating will do him fine if he doesn't try to do too much out there, but he could stand to add a step. He'll suit up for Providence next season and looks like the type of blueliner who'll benefit greatly from the physicality of the college game.

Calvin Petersen

Goalie – Waterloo (USHL)
Born Oct 19, 1994 - Waterloo, IA
Height 6.01 - Weight 175 - Catches R

Games	Wins	Losses	GAA	Save%	SO
35	21	11	2.98	.906	3

Petersen is a massive goaltender for the Waterloo Blackhawks. He is very effective at eliminating the bottom half of the net and is great at using his long legs to shutdown backdoor scoring chances. He shows good lateral movement and is rarely beat with a deke in tight. Cal does go down into the butterfly quick at times and needs to work at standing tall to take away the top half of the net as well. He is good at going from the butterfly to the standing position quickly and hugs the post tight stopping most wraparound situations. He is good at getting out of his net to stop pucks being dumped in from wrapping around for his defenseman and shows the ability to move pucks up the ice when given time and space. Petersen does need to work on improving his rebound control but is generally good at making the first save.

Gabriel Paquin-Boudreau

LW – Baie Comeau(QMJHL)
Born Feb 21, 1995 – Beloeil, QC
Height 5.11 - Weight 167 – Shoots L

Games	Goals	Assists	PTS	PIMS	+/-
67	22	41	63	43	+31

He is fairly slight player at only 160 pounds so his effectiveness is by playing a really smart hockey game based on his playmaking abilities and great hockey sense. He anticipates where passes are going and positions himself well to intercept plays. He has above-average skating abilities and puck handling skills, effectively bringing the puck in neutral zone. His wrist shot is good and very accurate, but he doesn't use it nearly enough, preferring the passing game. His smarts serve him well again in his own zone, using a great positional game and strong awareness to be effective. Gabriel Paquyn-Boudreau is not a big player thus making him an average on the boards. He's also not an aggressive player, rarely recording hits He can get pushed off the puck by bigger defensemen and will need to bulk up before he plays professional hockey. He will also need to build consistency and a work ethic. We've seen him have some tremendous shifts energy wise, while minutes later he's gliding and looking disinterested on the ice. He needs to get his competitiveness elevated on some nights and keep moving his feet to be an effective player.

Stephen Harper

LW – Erie Otters (OHL)
Born March 25, 1995 - Hamilton, ON
Height 6.01 - Weight 200 - Shoots R

Games	Goals	Assists	Points	PIMS	+/-
67	18	20	38	24	-38

Stephen generally lives and dies on the ice by his two strongest attributes. He is a very smooth skater who is able to fly up and down the ice. He also has a very powerful shot which he is able to unload quickly and with power. Stephen has also shown a physical side. He's delivered some solid hits in our viewings but isn't one to drop the gloves or spend much time in the penalty box. Stephen was generally used on the point of the Otters power play due to his big shot. He was able to unload one-timers and get shots through traffic to create rebounds and occasionally score. Unfortunately he needs to be a little more accurate with his shot and more precise with his decisions to shoot and pass. Ultimately our biggest concern with Stephen has been his decision making process. He can be a little risky with the puck at times and mistakes can go back the other way. We would also like to see him show more hustle in order to get back defensively. He put forward adequate numbers, but not what we expected out of him considering his skill set.

Cole Cassels

Center – Oshawa Generals (OHL)
Born May 4, 1995 – Columbus, OH
Height 6.00 - Weight 178 - Shoots R

Games	Goals	Assists	Points	PIMS	+/-
64	15	28	42	61	+7

Cole was a regular on Oshawa's third line consistently received top penalty killing minutes and was very strong in this role. Any team looking at selecting Cole will likely look primarily to his ability to shut down the opposition. He constantly maintains excellent defensive zone positioning and gets his sticks in lanes. He's willing to get down and block shots and pressures the puck carrier very well. He also engages regularly in battles. Cole has really improved his skating ability over the last two years and he's turned this area into an asset to his game. He wins races to a lose puck and can carry it deep into the offensive zone. He engages in puck battles in all three zones, however, has experienced mixed results in this area primarily due to a lack of strength. Offensively he doesn't appear to have a great amount of upside at the pro level. Many of his plays around the goal area with the puck revolve around throwing the puck into the slot and hoping for the best, and he doesn't show a very high level of puck skills. He has shown some moves on the breakaway, and gets many of his goals around the slot. We see Cole being a penalty killing specialist who plays a bottom six role, should he make the next level.

Kayle Doetzel

Defense – Red Deer (WHL)
Born June 19, 1995 - Saskatoon
Height 6.02 - Weight 190 - Shoots R

HOCKEYPROSPECT.COM

DRAFT GUIDE'13

Games	Goals	Assists	Points	PIMS	+/-
49	0	6	6	20	-4

Doetzel is known for his work in the defensive zone. He provides a physical presence at all times, and is difficult to play against along the wall. He is constantly in good position to protect the slot from dangerous situations. He is more than willing to take a hit to make a play with the puck when there is forecheck pressure, and is very strong on his skates. Doetzel is able to stay on his feet with the puck and quickly get the puck out of trouble. Offensively, Doetzel will probably never regularly put up points, but has the ability to make good passes out of the zone. However, he can at times rush plays off the glass instead of making the smart pass. He also does a good job of pinching down the walls when necessary to keep the offensive pressure going. Teams looking for a dependable defenseman for the future will take a long look at Doetzel. He has the size to take on big forwards at the pro level, and the potential defensively to at least be a bottom pairing defenseman if he continues to work on his skating abilities and poise with the puck.

Jake Guentzel

Center - SIOUX CITY (USHL)
Born Oct 6, 1994 – Omaha, NE
Height 5.09 - Weight 157 - Shoots L

HOCKEYPROSPECT.COM

DRAFT GUIDE'13

Games	Goals	Assists	Points	PIMS	+/-
60	29	44	73	24	+13

Jake Guentzel had an incredibly impressive 73 points in 60 games this season being named USHL rookie of the year. Guentzel was a dangerous offensive force every time he stepped on the ice and he is a player who has really nice hands and moves to skate the puck up the ice on an end-to-end rush then can make a great pass to move the puck to a man driving hard to the net for a great opportunity in tight. He protects the puck really well along the boards. His hands are incredible and the ability to find lanes to move the puck unmatched. He is not scared or intimidated to drive the puck to the net and he opens up so well to take passes and provide his teammates with scoring options. He has great offensive instincts to get to the slot, find space and open up for passes and he also has the vision and ability to get the puck to the right areas. Guentzel is a smaller forward which will make it difficult for him moving forward and he therefore needs to add size and strength if he ever wants to play at the next level. Jake is committed to join the University of Nebraska-Omaha this fall of 2013.

Sergey Tolchinsky

LW– Soo Greyhounds (OHL)
Born Feb 3, 1995 - Russia
Height 5.07 - Weight 152 - Shoots L

HOCKEYPROSPECT.COM DRAFT GUIDE'13

Games	Goals	Assists	Points	PIMS	+/-
62	26	25	51	12	+8

Tolchinsky is an undersized forward with exceptional skating ability. Sergey is a dynamic player who can stickhandle in a phone booth and score highlight reel goals. He is very shifty and shows good awareness also showing creativity in one on one situations and has a strong inside move cutting to the slot before putting pucks on net. Tolchinsky has a tendency to try to do too much on his own and would benefit from moving the puck to his line mates creating more space for him to skate in the open. The majority of his rushes end up in the corner of the offensive zone and more than half the time does not result in solid scoring chances. Sergey plays with a shoot first mentality and does have a strong wrist shot that fools goaltenders with a quick release. Tolchinsky had a solid playoff and was great ath the IIHF World U18 Championships. Sergey projects to be a top six or bust type of player. He is not suited whatsoever for the bottom six role and will need to play an offensive role at the NHL level in order to make it to that level.

Felix Girard

Centre – Baie Comeau (QMJHL)
Born May 9,1994 – Cap-Rouge
Height 5.11 - Weight 190 - Shoots R

HOCKEYPROSPECT.COM DRAFT GUIDE'13

Games	Goals	Assists	Points	PIMS	+/-
58	23	38	61	58	+18

Girard plays with a rarely seen intensity and his natural enthusiasm leads by example. In our numerous viewings, we have never seen Félix Girard get outworked in any area on the ice. He wins his battles, completes every check, plays a tremendous "in your face" type of game and is very good at getting under the skin of players. Not a really tall player at 5'11", but considerably big and strong. Girard has no fear and won't give an inch to even the biggest of opponents. He is the kind of player you want on the ice against the opposition's top players. He will make these players pay the price and will get them off their game. Defensively, Girard is outstanding, winning the important face offs, laying down in front of shots, blocking passing lanes with a smart stick positioning and paying attention to the details. He's always the first forward back and always comes in hard on support for his teammates. He keeps his head up on a swivel, staying well aware of what's around him, reading and reacting displaying intelligence defensively. His explosiveness could improve as he gains speed, which will benefit him in hitting his opponents, as relentless as they are at the next level.

Cole Ully

LW – Kamloops Blazers (WHL)
Born Feb 20, 1995 – Calgary, AB
Height 6.00 - Weight 164 - Shoots L

HOCKEYPROSPECT.COM DRAFT GUIDE '13

Games	Goals	Assists	Points	PIMS	+/-
62	22	28	50	37	+27

Cole Ully is a very good two-way forward who has stepped up his game immensely at both ends of the ice and his development has really soared this year. He is always on the pursuit of loose pucks, and quickly joins the rush off the wing to provide another option. When he handles the puck, he looks loose and smooth as he works through traffic. He identifies open lanes quickly, and shifts his direction to attack any open seams. The one area of improvement for his game would be his ability to get shots off quickly from the slot. Ully takes too long to release his shots when he is covered, and lacks the size to be able to protect the puck and his stick from opponents to prevent them from disrupting his shots. Defensively, Ully is a good penalty killer who has a very good stick. He is skilled at intercepting passes, always being in the right position to do so. He is fearless when it comes to blocking shots, and is willing to take a hit to make a play along the boards. His game projects well as a 3rd line winger with a scoring touch at the pro level.

Brent Pedersen

LW – Kitchener Rangers (OHL)
Born July 5 1995 – Kitchener, ON
Height 6.02 - Weight 205 - Shoots L

HOCKEYPROSPECT.COM DRAFT GUIDE '13

Games	Goals	Assists	Points	PIMS	+/-
67	14	16	30	52	+11

Pederson has shown improved skating throughout this year with size and a heavy shot. Pedersen reads the ice well enough to effectively use his teammates. He showed flashes of offensive creativity when given the opportunity to play with more skilled line mates. Brent works hard in the offensive zone and is good at using his size shielding opponents from the puck with his body before cutting to the net. He is big enough to withstand a beating in front of the net and is constantly looking for rebound opportunities. He is good at using his size to create space for his line mates and can add a physical side to his game when needed. Pedersen will be looked upon to have a much larger role in the Ranger offense next season and will look to build off of a solid sophomore season. At the pro level he's projected to be a power forward who is able to produce offensively to a limited extent. He looks very prototypical as a power forward and understands himself and his role very well. He needs to continue to improve skating and work on getting even stronger to be able to be more dominant along the walls and while driving the net.

Josh Burnside

LW – Mississauga Steelheads (OHL)
Born Feb 11, 1995 – Brampton, ON
Height 5.11 - Weight 171 - Shoots L

Games	Goals	Assists	Points	PIMS	+/-
68	12	16	28	22	-13

Burnside possesses great speed. He is really quick when he gets going and very willing to bring a net-front presence on the power play. He hustles well in both ends of the ice, can cycle the puck effectively and then gets himself to the front of the net to try to create chances from in tight. Burnside has also shown good offensive instincts to acquire good position in the offensive zone. He can read the play to determine when the opposition's defense are giving him a bit too much space, which allows him to make a play. He is willing to go to the dirty areas, competes well for the puck and plays the game with a good energy and compete level. He needs to work on his puck control as he often appears to be playing on the edge mishandles it at times. Moving forward he will need to continue to show a responsible 200 foot game, where he can be effective offensively and contribute on a nightly basis, but at the same time take care of business in his own end and not be a liability.

Will Butcher

Defense – USNTDP (USHL)
Born Jan 6, 1995 – Sun Prairie, USA
Height 5.09 - Weight 191 - Shoots L

Games	Goals	Assists	Points	PIMS	+/-
57	9	20	29	6	+15

Will possesses great skating and puck skills, able to accelerate from his zone into open space up ice with poise and navigate neutral zone traffic. He deals well with forecheck pressure and is smart about making safe plays to clear the zone when necessary, but can kick start the offense by head manning the puck with crisp feeds. He isn't afraid to take hits to make plays with the puck. Thanks to quick feet and good awareness, he's good at keeping the puck in the zone at the point. He can snap the puck with a quick release and precise accuracy. Also has a good one-timer that he's unafraid to use. His defensive play is mixed. He keeps his stick active and tracks the play with his head up, but sometimes has trouble finding the middle ground between overaggressive and passive positioning. Even when he does read the play correctly and plays the body, he lacks the strength to be effective on the boards and in front of the net against bigger players.

Tobias Liljendahl

Center – DJURGARDEN JR. (SWE)
Born Jan 10, 1995 – Stockholm, SWE
Height 6.01 - Weight 214 - Shoots R

HOCKEYPROSPECT.COM
DRAFT GUIDE' 13

Games	Goals	Assists	Points	PIMS	+/-
29	4	6	10	4	+1

Tobias plays a pretty simple game. He is a two-way centre who can be used in both offensive and defensive situations. He shows great hockey sense making smart plays with the puck and displays excellent positioning and constantly seems to be where he should be. He doesn't try to force plays and will just choose the smart option with the puck. He also has a powerful shot with a quick release. He can play physical but he isn't overly aggressive and will also use his size to protect the puck. Tobias showed excellent defensively in different situations including penalty kills and was chosen to be the lone forward on a 5 on 3 kill. His calm, never risky demeanor really serves him well on the penalty kill. He quickly gets into good positioning, gets in passing lanes, blocks shot and does a great job in these situations. His top speed is not bad at all for a player his size but his first few steps need work to get him to where he needs to be. We feel Tobias is more well suited for a bottom six role and thus may go later in the draft.

David Pope

LW – West Kelowna (BCHL)
Born Sept 27, 1994 – Edmonton, AB
Height 6.02 - Weight 187 - Shoots L

HOCKEYPROSPECT.COM
DRAFT GUIDE' 13

Games	Goals	Assists	Points	PIMS	+/-
42	17	22	39	20	N/A

Pope is a big, skilled winger who plays a good all-around game. He provided match-up problems for opponents because of his mix of skill and size. Pope is at his best when he is moving his feet and attacking the middle of the ice. He can create a lot of scoring chances by skating down the wing. Pope has a good slap shot, and is set up to use it on the PP consistently. However he needs to be more accurate. Pope also needs to be a more consistent factor in games. Pope is also not very good along the walls, especially given his size. His desire to win puck battles is not very high, and he gets beat for pucks time and time again. He needs to develop a mean streak in his game to be successful. Defensively, Pope is adequate without the puck. He does a good job of maintaining position to limit chances for opposing defensemen. Ultimately, David was able to rely on his skill at the BCHL level but won't get away with it at higher levels and will need to adding more grit and consistent work ethic to his game.

Jerret Smith

Defense – Seattle Thunderbirds (WHL)
Born April 1, 1995 – Surrey, BC
Height 6.01 - Weight 198 - Shoots R

Games	Goals	Assists	Points	PIMS	+/-
71	1	19	20	33	-22

Smith is a good defensive defenseman who is developing into a good shut down defenseman for the future. He started the season quite raw, but received consistent ice time and has since really improved his overall game. He gives very little opportunities in the slot, and he is quite good at picking off passes and knocking away pucks as opponents come down his wing on the rush. Smith is solid along the walls, and really gives opponents very little to work with. He could work on being more physical in front of the net and be a tougher presence to play against. His gap control also needs work because of his lack of foot speed. He gives opponents some room to come into the zone, and is not able to close the gap and land a good hit on them. Offensively, Smith will probably never develop into a dependable offensive player. He needs to work on handling the puck in pressure and make good outlet passes. His play with the puck is quite mediocre, and it is definitely something that he will have to fix.

Danny Vanderwiel

LW – Plymouth Whalers (OHL)
Born Feb 17, 1995 – Island Lake, IL
Height 6.00 - Weight 210 - Shoots L

Games	Goals	Assists	Points	PIMS	+/-
57	4	10	14	41	-1

Despite a lack of ice on a stacked Plymouth team he never quit working. He always competed extremely hard and was like a big ball of energy in all of our viewings. Vanderwiel is an energetic physical winger who plays every moment of every shift at full speed. He hits hard in open ice and along the boards. Whenever there is an opportunity to finish a check he takes it. He always wins more than his share of battles along the wall. He also forces turnovers helping his team generate puck control and he cycles the puck intelligently. Danny is very solid positionally in all three zones and we saw him grow as one of Plymouth's best penalty killers due to this. He's willing to sacrifice himself for his team. At times while even strength he almost looked like he was the third defenseman for the Whalers going deep into the zone and doing his best to shut down the opposition. He's a fairly effective skater for his size. His offensive upside is not very high and he doesn't show signs of growing into an offensive talent. However Vanderwiel seems to know exactly who he is and what he needs to do to make the NHL. He's an energetic, lunch pail grinder type of player who plays bottom six minutes and kills penalties.

Eamon McAdam

Goalie– Waterloo (USHL)
Born Sept 24, 1994 – Doylestown, PA
Height 6.02 - Weight 188 - Catches L

HOCKEYPROSPECT.COM
DRAFT GUIDE '13

Games	Wins	Losses	GAA	Save %	SO
31	17	9	3.45	.896	2

Eamon got his developmental push out of Team Comcast in 2009-2010 where he made the jump to the junior hockey ranks splitting time between the USHL's Waterloo Blackhawks and the NAHL's Austin Bruins. Eamon received a fair amount of starts for a player who was just 16 to start the season in 2011-2012 and increased his starts again this year getting a lot of exposure and recognition early hanks to his participation at the Junior Club World Cup in August. Eamon has proven to cover the lower part of the net very well. He gets around post to post moderately well and shows good second effort on rebounds. He struggles a little with high shots because he has a tendency to go down a little too early. McAdam also benefitted from playing at the World Jr. A Challenge. Eamon is slated to join Penn State University this fall of 2013.

Rinat Valiyev

Defense – Indiana Ice (USHL)
Born May 11, 1995 – Russia
Height 6.01 - Weight 190 - Shoots L

HOCKEYPROSPECT.COM
DRAFT GUIDE '13

Games	Goals	Assists	Points	PIMS	+/-
36	6	7	13	43	-6

The Russian blueliner made the jump to North American hockey this year with Indiana, and showed well with the team despite their last place finish. He plays a sound two-way game with plenty of upside. His defensive game is strong with an intelligent, active stick and tight coverage. He's not a bruiser but he plays physical and closes gaps quickly. His positioning, especially against the rush, is excellent. He had an excellent showing for Russia at the Five Nations U18 tournament, where he led all defensemen in scoring. He makes a good first pass but can also carry the puck when given a lane. He's an excellent skater and, while he doesn't project as a top pairing power play defenseman as a professional, can quarterback the man advantage well. He pinches and joins the rush at the right times, and shows a good wrister with smart placement, either shooting to score or aiming for tips and rebounds. He doesn't have a booming shot but it's still effective. He can rush the puck and does well to evade fore checkers, but makes the safe play under pressure if necessary. He suffered a season-ending injury in February, which may affect his stock come draft time, but there's a lot to like about his polished and responsible play.

J.C. Lipon

RW – Kamloops Blazers (WHL)
Born July 10, 1993 – Regina, SK
Height 5.11 - Weight 180 - Shoots R

HOCKEYPROSPECT.COM

Games	Goals	Assists	Points	PIMS	+/-
61	36	53	89	115	+34

JC the 2011 and 2012 NHL Entry Drafts, but has gained a lot of attention this season especially after joining Team Canada for the World Junior Championships. Offensively, Lipon just seems to be in the right place at the right time on a consistent basis. He always seems to be around the puck and battles hard for loose pucks on the forecheck and continues the attack for his team. Lipon is not a particularly gifted scorer or playmaker, but seems to be comfortable in both roles. Lipon is one of the most dependable penalty killers on the Blazers. He is always out in crucial situations, and really covers his side of the ice well and quickly reads the play and get into proper positioning. He is quite intelligent without the puck, and is not afraid to block shots and dish out hits to get the puck back for his team. One area of concern in Lipon's game Is his undisciplined play. He is prone to taking penalties after the whistle, and plays like a pest out on the ice. He is quick to retaliate and has a tough time keeping his composure.

Dylan Labbe

Defense – Shawinigan (QMJHL)
Born Jan 9, 1995 – St. George , PQ
Height 6.01 - Weight 108 - Shoots L

HOCKEYPROSPECT.COM

Games	Goals	Assists	Points	PIMS	+/-
61	7	21	28	57	-40

He likes to carry the puck and is really confident when starting the breakout on his own. His puck handling abilities are good, he can make his way around players easily with slick moves, displaying confidence when bringing the puck up. He will rarely lose handling of the puck and can maneuver comfortably in traffic. His forward speed for a 6,02 189 pounds player is great, using long powerful strides to reach top speed quickly, which helps him get away from pressure and start transition effectively. His shot is tremendous, powerful and accurate, preferring a great release with the wrist shot to a slapshot. He got numerous scoring chances with the hard wrister on the powerplay this season, but needs to put more pucks on net 5-on-5. His passing game is also above-average, finding teammates easily and quickly in the offensive zone with hard passes on tape. He was used on the powerplay for the vast majority of the season and showed a nice puck-moving potential. We like the physical attributes Labbé possess, being able to play a physical game down-low, rarely getting beat in restricted areas. We like to see him play with an aggressive edge, something he didn't do with enough consistency this season. Labbé has an attractive toolbox with the size and his existing abilities.

Robin Norell

Defense – DJURGARDEN JR. (SWE)
Born Feb 18, 1995 – Stockholm, SWE
Height 5.11 - Weight 189 - Shoots L

HOCKEYPROSPECT.COM

Games	Goals	Assists	Points	PIMS	+/-
33	1	4	5	4	+16

Robin is a simple, stocky defenseman who plays a strong defensive game. He's solid in his own end, playing a positional game with an active stick and intelligent contact. He understands the limitations of his size and waits for the right opportunity to play the body, rather than trying to overpower with brute force. He can make big hits standing up at the blueline and his repertoire includes a great hip check. He's sturdy on his feet and though not the strongest skater, positions himself well enough that he rarely has to move quickly to recover. He makes safe outlets and can occasionally stretch the rink with long bomb passes, but tends to keep it pretty simple with the puck and knows when to chip it off the glass and out. He has stretches of over aggressiveness and puck troubles, but for the most part is safe and reliable.

Tyler Lewington

Defense – Medicine Hat (WHL)
Born Dec 5, 1994 – Edmonton, AB
Height 6.01 - Weight 189 - Shoots R

HOCKEYPROSPECT.COM

Games	Goals	Assists	Points	PIMS	+/-
69	2	24	26	131	+14

Lewington is a puck moving defenseman who plays a simple game. He is quite poised with the puck, and is able to escape forechecks and quickly move the puck up to his forwards. Lewington is a competent skater who does not overwhelm opponents with his speed, but does an admirable job carrying the puck. Lewington however does not possess a very good shot. Defensively, Lewington is quite inconsistent. There are times when he uses his stick well to knock away pucks and pick off passes, than there are times when he looks like he has bad habits in his own zone, and not be as strong on the puck and on opponents with his body as he could be. There are also times when he is caught out of position and gives up scoring chances in tight. He has to use his body more to block shots and be tougher to play against along the walls. Lewington could become a useful player as a pro one day, but his play without the puck will have to improve immensely. He has to be more consistently effective, and put in the effort to provide more impact in his own end.

Zach Hall

Center – Barrie Colts (OHL)
Born April 29, 1993 – Belleville, ON
Height 5.10 - Weight 172 - Shoots L

Games	Goals	Assists	Points	PIMS	+/-
63	24	57	81	38	+9

Zach is being featured by us for a third straight season entering his final year of NHL Draft eligibility. Zach once again showed great improvements, this time leading the Barrie Colts in scoring during the regular season. Zach has shown his durability playing both center and wing. He has excellent speed and absorbs contact well, eluding checkers. He's good with the puck and shows the knowledge of when to pass and when to shoot. Zach is likely to be drafted late in this draft due to his potential. If he is not, then we fully expect an NHL team to give him a long look as he is eligible to play in the AHL next year.

Alexander Henriksson

LW – FARJESTAD JR. (SWE)
Born Feb 7, 1995 – Skovee, SWE
Height 6.02 - Weight 190 - Shoots R

Games	Goals	Assists	Points	PIMS	+/-
41	9	7	16	30	+8

Alexander has developed up through the Skovde IK club early in his career playing in a J20 league as a 14 year old but eventually moved over to the more established Farjestad program working his way up starting with the J18 eventually joining the J20 full time. Alexander is a threat in the offensive zone primarily due to his shot. He utilizes his size well when driving the puck into the zone protecting it and taking it to the net. He forechecks hard and can force turnovers and finish some checks taking the puck away and turning it into a chance. Alexander just needs to play this game more consistently. While he has offensive skills, we're not convinced to this point he'll turn into a big offensive producer. However he does show some abilities that could translate to him playing a support role forechecking and chipping in offensively.

Frederik Tiffels

LW – Muskegon (USHL)
Born May 20, 1995 – Cologne, GER
Height 6.00 - Weight 185 - Shoots L

HOCKEYPROSPECT.COM

Games	Goals	Assists	Points	PIMS	+/-
50	3	22	25	10	+13

Tiffels was picked in the 2nd round, 17th overall by the Muskegon Lumberjacks and came to the USHL from Germany to play in 50 games for the Lumberjacks registering 25 points. Tiffels plays with good speed and agility and will hustle to get on loose pucks, using his body to protect it and get a good cycle going in deep in the offensive zone. He can move the puck very effectively, possesses exceptional vision and passing and brings good speed to the game as well. He likes to come down the wing with speed on the outside, protects the puck well but the most noticeable attribute of this player by far is his passing. He has vision to see all his options, is creative, can read the play well and guys himself time before moving the puck. He plays the game with an element of physicality, but still needs to get stronger on the puck along the boards. Tiffels also needs to work on shooting the puck more often.

Brody Silk

Center– Sudbury Wolves (OHL)
Born Nov 30, 1994 – Iroquois, ON
Height 6.00 - Weight 185 - Shoots L

HOCKEYPROSPECT.COM

Games	Goals	Assists	Points	PIMS	+/-
55	12	24	36	102	-5

Brody has really progressed each year as he was used very limited at 16 however his role increased as he entered his second season. Then he became a key two-way player for Sudbury wearing the "A" in his 3rd year. He finished the year with 36 points and 102 penalty minutes in 55 games showing that offensive potential with an aggression and edge as well. He possesses pretty good size and uses it to cycle the puck and go hard to the net for opportunities from in tight. He keeps his game simple, competes for the puck and challenges the point well. He can make good short passes and is a pretty good skater with a good first 3 steps for a quick acceleration. He gets to the front of the net and is not intimidated to play in those dirty areas and the coach likes to use him in critical situations, probably for this reason. Silk's best chance for success is to continue establishing himself as a solid defensively responsible forward that kills penalties, does the dirty work on the ice, battles and competes hard for the puck and can be an asset for a team moving forward. He may not have the most skill but seems to understand the game well, uses good positioning and instincts in all three zones.

Thomas Aldworth

RW – Cushing Academy (HS USA)
Born April 30, 1995 – Brownsville,TN
Height 5.11 - Weight 179 - Shoots R

HOCKEYPROSPECT.COM

DRAFT GUIDE'13

Games	Goals	Assists	Points	PIMS	+/-
31	10	17	27	8	-2

The lanky, Texas-bred winger plays the game the right way, skating well and involving himself in the play at both ends of the rink. He plays with a lot of intensity, especially with the puck where he gets up to speed quickly and can beat defenders with deft stick handling or brute strength down the outside. He protects the puck well and shows off an excellent wrist shot that he releases deceptively, though he could stand to shoot more. He forechecks and back checks with vigor and takes the body hard. He's aggressive and capably defensively with a good compete level along the boards and strong penalty killing. He does too much at times with the puck, trying to make fancy plays instead of putting it on net or taking the easy pass, which can cause him problems. His tools and skill set are suited to the professional game, and he has the frame to be a force when he bulks up.

Antoine Bibeau

Goalie – PEI Rockets (QMJHL)
Born May 1, 1994 – Victoriaville,PQ
Height 6.02 - Weight 207 - Catches L

HOCKEYPROSPECT.COM

DRAFT GUIDE'13

Games	Wins	Losses	GAA	Save %	SO
46	28	11	2.81	.911	5

Antoine is a big kid, taking out tons of space in front of his net. For a goalie his size, his athleticism and flexibility is impressive, he made a lot of spectacular saves in our viewings of him. He is a quick and agile goalie, butterfly based but his technique is not his strongest asset and he will rely on reflexes to make saves, even some that are easier than they look to be. He has quick hands and although he is quick on knees sometimes his reactions are accurate and quick with the glove. Bibeau likes to be aggressive, challenge shooters and obviously that's when he is at his best and most confident. Bibeau's biggest weakness is his work ethic during a game, sometimes will get lazy in his positioning, will over move and rely too much on his reflexes to make saves. His angle coverage, butterfly base positioning and rebound control will get inaccurate and pucks will get through him because of that. He certainly has some natural physical abilities that are interesting, but for us it remains to be seen if he can keep the same kind of confidence and level of performances that he had this season with PEI with the low level of work ethic we've seen.

Leon Bristedt

RW – LINKOPING JR. (SWE)
Born March 14,1995 – Stockholm
Height 5.07.5 - Weight 180 - Shoots L

Games	Goals	Assists	Points	PIMS	+/-
31	9	13	22	49	+11

Leon is an undersized yet ultra talented and competitive forward who is very creative offensively with the puck. He has the ability to elude multiple defenders but also possesses a calm and patience with the puck that allows him to create plays for his teammates. He also has the ability to possess the puck for long periods of times, evading checkers, sometimes forcing them to take a stick or holding infraction just to slow him down. Bristedt also will drive the net hard with the puck and try to finish himself. He has a powerful shot and lets to let it go in the offensive zone. Leon is sometimes one of, if not the smallest player on the ice. He overcomes this regularly with a tremendous work ethic, tenacious energy and a never quit attitude. Defensively he gets all over the puck carrier and is capable of forcing turnovers. Leon is the type of player NHL teams would love to have, but wished he was much bigger. There's concern about his 5'8" frame, but little to no concern about his skill set or competitiveness.

Matthew Murphy

Defense –Halifax Mooseheads (QMJHL)
Born May 1, 1995 – Fredericton, NB
Height 6.02 - Weight 197 - Shoots L

Games	Goals	Assists	Points	PIMS	+/-
69	2	31	33	36	+20

Matt Murphy has shown the two sides of his game this season, one where he makes poor decisions and is all about offense, will join the rush and cause multiple turnovers carelessly. The good side of Murphy is when he plays a cautious game, waiting for the right times to rush the puck and effectively uses his skating skills. He has good skating abilities for his size, but could work on his explosiveness as he can be beat by quick skaters going out wide. His top speed is impressive and he has displayed the great forward speed he possesses multiple times when rushing the puck. Murphy will play a punishing physical game at times, but has lacked consistency in this area over the whole season. Murphy has a pretty good shot that he doesn't release enough from the blue line, especially when he can set it up on the one-timer. A confident puckhandler, Murphy prefers to pass the puck and use his offensive awareness to find teammates. While we like the offensive potential, we feel Murphy's work in his defensive zone is still just average. He has progressed nicely with the Mooseheads in the 2nd half of the season, but his defensive hockey sense still is lacking. He will make poor decisions with the puck and will be aggressive at the wrong times.

Alex Kile

HOCKEYPROSPECT.COM

DRAFT GUIDE' 13

LW– Green Bay Gamblers (USHL)
Born July 9, 1994 – Troy, MI
Height 5.11 - Weight 190 - Shoots L

Games	Goals	Assists	Points	PIMS	+/-
56	30	30	60	60	+8

After showing some intriguing flashes of talent last year, Alex really took his game to another level and was a key player for the Gamblers all season long. Alex developed through the Detroit Honeybaked system after joining the USHL's Green Bay Gamblers for the 2011-2012 season. Alex handles the puck very well and displays intriguing creativity with the puck at this level he is capable of creating offense for himself and his teammates. He also has a fairly effective shot. Alex isn't an overly physical player but will finish his checks and displays a willingness to battle. Alex is a re-entry player for the 2013 NHL Entry Draft and has a chance of being drafted. Alex has a very tough decision to make next season. He was selected in the 2010 OHL Priority Selection Draft by the London Knights.

Trevor Moore

HOCKEYPROSPECT.COM

DRAFT GUIDE' 13

LW – Tri City Storm (USHL)
Born March 31,1995–Thousand Oaks, CA
Height 5.09 - Weight 170 - Shoots L

Games	Goals	Assists	Points	PIMS	+/-
62	20	43	63	26	-20

Trevor is a flashy offensive talent with good skating and puck skills. He's an excellent stick handler and uses his quickness to dart around defenders, though lacks the extra gear that you'd like to see for a player of his stature and he can be weak on the puck against heavy coverage. His offensive zone positioning is solid and he is able to find soft spots in coverage to get open for shots, but has a hard time fighting for position in front of the net due to his lack of strength. He shoots the puck well with hard, accurate wrister shots and one-timers. He frequently tries to do too much by himself with the puck. His defensive game needs work, but he's active on the forecheck with a good stick and shows decent penalty killing positioning. Despite his strength he has also finished some checks effectively. Though he's an excellent junior forward, he hasn't shown that he has the evasiveness necessary to project him as a major scoring threat at the NHL level.

Sean Malone

Center – USNTDP (USHL)
Born April 30, 1995- Buffalo, NY
Height 5.11 - Weight 183 - Shoots L

Games	Goals	Assists	Points	PIMS	+/-
44	13	14	27	19	+12

Sean plays a gritty style suited to a depth role, but his offensive game has shown gradual improvement. He's strong in front of the net in the offensive zone and fights for rebounds and loose pucks, as well as taking the pucks to the crease and fighting to score until the whistle blows. He's good at screening the goaltender and redirecting pucks. He also shows finesse from time to time with skill moves, but for the most part keeps things pretty simple. Though he's an average skater, he's strong on his feet and has a good motor that keeps him involved in the play. He forechecks, back checks, and shows the willingness to get involved physically, taking the body defensively and taking hits to make plays with the puck. He lacks dynamic enough hands and feet to project him as a real offensive threat at the professional level. He has the aggressiveness to be an NHL bottom-six player, he lacks ideal size or speed for that role.

Ty Stanton

Defense – Medicine Hat (WHL)
Born May 23, 1995 – St. Albert, AB
Height 6.03 - Weight 170 - Shoots L

Games	Goals	Assists	Points	PIMS	+/-
44	2	14	16	29	-6

Stanton is a skilled defenseman who brought a good offensive presence for the Tigers in the backend when he was in the lineup. He was bothered by small injuries throughout the year, which has affected his development. The best asset of Stanton is probably his puck moving abilities. He makes very good passes from the backend to get the attack going for his team. He has the ability to carry the puck up the ice to provide another threat off the rush, and makes good decisions with the puck. He walks the blue line quite well to create some space to get a shot off, but he is definitely more of a passer than a shooter. Defensively, Stanton definitely has to get much stronger. He gets pushed off the puck too easily, and does not win enough battles along the walls. He needs to add muscle to his height to have a chance of playing as a pro one day. Stanton shows above average skating abilities, and will have to keep improving his use of his reach to keep opponents to the outside. He is quite soft to play against, and will have to provide a more physical presence in games.

Mitchell Wheaton

Defense – Kelowna Rockets (WHL)
Born Feb 6, 1995 – Sherwood Park
Height 6.04 - Weight 228 - Shoots L

HOCKEYPROSPECT.COM

DRAFT GUIDE' 13

Games	Goals	Assists	Points	PIMS	+/-
39	1	7	8	27	+20

Wheaton is a big defensive defenseman who stepped into the Rockets' line up this season and provided a solid presence in the backend. Wheaton possesses a good stick and the ability to be in good position to cover a lot of area to try to prevent good scoring chances. He uses his long reach to his advantage and does a good job to knocking away pucks and keeping opponents to the outside. He is very strong along the boards, and his physical abilities seem to be ready for the pro level already. Offensively, Wheaton's game is quite limited. His outlet passes are average, and has shown limited playmaking abilities. He has an average shot and he is not particularly good at walking the line to get shots through traffic. Wheaton will also need to work on his skating abilities. He is good at quick starts and stops along the corner, but his overall speed will need to be improved to be more effective on the rush at the professional level. He has had some troubles with keeping quick players to the outside at the junior level as well.

Tyler Hill

LW – Chicago Steele (USHL)
Born April 13, 1995 – Hamilton,ON
Height 6.06 - Weight 220 - Shoots L

HOCKEYPROSPECT.COM

DRAFT GUIDE' 13

Games	Goals	Assists	Points	PIMS	+/-
30	6	6	12	34	+10

The hulking forward has shown flashes of greatness, but has yet to develop consistency. He can use his long reach and frame to protect the puck well and is surprisingly shifty for his size with good agility and excellent hands, but doesn't always utilize his abilities. He floats too often and has a hard time carrying the puck against physical checking, especially at the USHL level this year where he lacked the first step quickness to. He has a hard, accurate wrist shot and he likes to put the puck on net from all over the offensive zone. He works well on the boards with his size and fights through checks though he lacks killer instinct overall. He can forecheck, back check, and penalty kill well. He can play mean and outright ragdoll opposing players, but mostly seems unwilling. He's an intriguing prospect based on his combination of skill, size, and speed, but is incredibly raw and may have actually hurt his stock by playing the second half of the season in the USHL. At the junior level, it became clear that despite his tools, he still has a ton of work to do before he can be considered a legitimate professional prospect.

Luke Ripley

Defense – Powell River (BCHL)
Born April 16, 1994 – Kitimat, BC
Height 6.03 - Weight 181 - Shoots L

HOCKEYPROSPECT.COM
DRAFT GUIDE' 13

Games	Goals	Assists	Points	PIMS	+/-
46	2	11	13	85	N/A

Ripley is a big, defensive defenseman who provides a physical presence from the backend. One area of weakness for Ripley is his footwork along the walls and agility. He needs to work on making quicker stops and being able to stick to opponents on the boards and not give them a lane to the net. He has been able to develop good overall speed, but his explosive quickness still needs to be improved on. He also needs to work on being in good position without the puck in the neutral zone so that opponents cannot go wide and have an easy lane to attack. There are times when he is caught standing still in the middle of the ice, and is not able to cut down the angle on an opponent attacking the net. The best asset of Ripley is his physicality. He dishes out hits often and is difficult to play against along the walls. He uses his long reach to poke away pucks and intercept passes consistently, and because of the improvements he made with his skating, these skills are much more noticeable as he is more often in the play to be able to make an impact.

Connor Rankin

LW – Tri City (WHL)
Born Nov 30, 1994 – North Vancouver
Height 6.00 - Weight 194 - Shoots L

HOCKEYPROSPECT.COM
DRAFT GUIDE' 13

Games	Goals	Assists	Points	PIMS	+/-
71	32	26	58	34	+9

Rankin is a good skater who can move quickly up the ice with the puck. He looks comfortable weaving through traffic, and limits his turnovers by quickly moving the puck when he senses trouble. He will never blow past any dependable defenseman with his speed and stick handling abilities, but will be able to push the defense on their heels and give teammates some room to work with and find some open areas out on the ice. He looked to be more of a playmaker in the previous seasons, but has shown that he has a scoring touch to his game and the ability to quickly catch and shoot the puck from anywhere out on the ice. Defensively, Rankin has shown that he could play a good 2 way game. He has developed good habits in his game, and back checks hard on any type of a counter attack. He is reliable on the PK and does an above average job of getting into shooting lanes. There are times when he gets on the wrong side of the play and needs to take a penalty to prevent a scoring chance. He will have to continue to improve on his overall game to be a serviceable pro one day.

Victor Ohman

Center – MODO JR. (SWE)
Born July 1, 1995 - Ornskoldsvik, SWE
Height 5.09 - Weight 170 - Shoots L

HOCKEYPROSPECT.COM

DRAFT GUIDE' 13

Games	Goals	Assists	Points	PIMS	+/-
37	9	15	24	12	+10

Victor has been the product of the MODO system for the past few years. He has taken his time working his way up starting with the J18 after a brief appearance at the U16 level and played primarily J18 the past two seasons. This year he played exclusively at the J20 level with a one game exception where he made his Elitserien debut. Ohman is a skilled offensive player who displays excellent skating ability and is able to create plays for himself and his linemates. He shows some clear flashes of offensive ability and even protects the puck well for his size. While he's strong offensively he struggles with both the physical side of the game and the defensive side of the game. While he can skate control and pass the puck well, showing distinctive offensive potential, he may be too far away in other areas of the game. A team may be intrigued by him later on in the draft.

Mackenzie Weegar

Defense – Halifax Mooseheads (USHL)
Born Jan 7, 1994 – Ottawa, ON
Height 5.11 - Weight 183 - Shoots R

HOCKEYPROSPECT.COM

DRAFT GUIDE' 13

Games	Goals	Assists	Points	PIMS	+/-
62	8	36	44	58	+55

Weegar is a 2-way defenseman, he was an asset all season long for the Mooseheads. He skates smoothly and follows the play really well. Weegar is a really smart player. With the puck, he sees the ice well and finds teammates easily on the breakout, making the transition very quickly. He has soft hands and can carry the puck himself to the neutral zone without issues. We like the poise and composure he shows when he has the puck on his stick, rarely making dumb decisions and waiting for the right moment before executing his play. Although he's a little undersized for a defenseman at 5-11, Weegar has several other tools to win the battles and make up for that downside. We've never seen him in trouble because of his size. He has a pretty accurate wrist shot but he's still tentative of using it instead waiting for a perfect opportunity. Without the puck, Weegar positions himself very well and will rarely lose his coverage. He blocks shots due to great positioning, his stick will take away space from the opposition. His footwork is good enough to follow most of the league's skaters, but should get better to play at the next level. He is dedicated and has a good work ethic.

Shane Kavanagh

RW – Cushing Academy (HS USA)
Born Jan 5, 1995- East Providence, RI
Height 5.11 - Weight 195 - Shoots R

Games	Goals	Assists	Points	PIMS	+/-
N/A	N/A	N/A	N/A	N/A	N/A

A sparkplug two-way forward with good hands and goal-scoring instincts, Kavanagh is well rounded and a nightmare to deal with. He has shifts were he outright lays out multiple players, sometimes even bigger guys who he has no business going after, much less overpowering. As a result, he gets targeted physically and can have some trouble dealing with serious contact. He plays with a lot of jump and is an excellent skater with a powerful stride. With the puck, he mostly plays a power forward game, taking the puck strong down the wing and hard to the net, which probably won't work for him much longer as he progresses to playing against bigger players, but he also possesses a great shot and can get open in the slot area. Has the tools to be an excellent two-way player and should be on the draft radar this year, though it's likely that he won't be selected.

Cameron Brace

Center – Owen Sound Attack (OHL)
Born April 8, 1993 – Markham,ON
Height 5.09.5 - Weight 176 - Shoots R

Games	Goals	Assists	Points	PIMS	+/-
66	35	39	74	74	+32

Brace has spent his entire four year OHL Career with the Attack. In that time he was a key part of his team winning the OHL Championship. He was a consistent point producer who provided work ethic this season looking very similar as he did last season. He is very speedy and quick. He is capable of driving the wing and taking some damage from defensemen while protecting the puck. Brace is more of a shooter than a passer and he has a quick release. He also has a knack for scoring big goals. He scored 10 goals, 7 in the first 10 games of the season. He also had three game winning goals just six games into the OHL season this year. Cameron may not be the biggest player in the ice, but he's not afraid to play physical or go head first into puck battles. What separates Brace from the average small, speedy goal scorer is his commitment to the defensive game. We've seen many occasions where Cameron has been willing to get down and block shots, where he's been a key contributor to the team's penalty kill, and he's come away with some short-handed goals thanks to his ability to force turnovers. Cameron is a player who we really feel may get drafted late. Should he go unselected, he should be pursued for an NHL camp invite.

Gage Ausmus

Defense – USNTDP (USHL)
Born April 22, 1995 – Billings, MT
Height 6.01 - Weight 211 - Shoots L

HOCKEYPROSPECT.COM DRAFT GUIDE '13

Games	Goals	Assists	Points	PIMS	+/-
56	2	10	12	48	+17

Gage has a habit of blending into the background, playing a steady game with smart defensive positioning and safe plays with the puck in his zone. Then, all of a sudden, he's laying a guy out at the blueline or pinching into the attack. One time this season, he jumped up and ended up with a shorthanded breakaway. These moments are fleeting and interspersed, and he sometimes goes a whole game without making himself noticeable. He's a smart player that picks his spots well. His end comes first, but if he sees a sure-thing opportunity to provide a little extra, he can do it. He lacks dynamic skating and puck skills, but seems to have a good handle on his limitations and knows how to keep things simple. He has the potential to be an NHL defenseman based on his humble approach and intelligence on the ice.

Stephen Nosad

RW – Peteborough Petes (OHL)
Born Jan 25,1995 – Tottenham, ON
Height 5.11 - Weight 188 - Shoots R

HOCKEYPROSPECT.COM DRAFT GUIDE '13

Games	Goals	Assists	Points	PIMS	+/-
62	10	9	19	6	-19

Stephen showed some very, very promising signs in his rookie season. He put together impressive point totals and put up almost a point per game for Team Ontario's World U-17 Challenge team. Nosad entered his NHL Draft Year on a high but this season was a step back for Stephen as he didn't quite elevate his game quite the way we expected. Stephen is one of those players who is capable of doing many things well, but nothing great. When he's on his game he shows off his skating ability and is willing to chase pucks into corners and battle hard winning more than his share of battles. He shows effective intelligence with the puck and knows when to pass or shoot. The concern with Stephen is he went through multiple stretches where we didn't feel he was working hard enough or playing his style of game. Regardless, we do believe Stephen could be selected late in this draft purely based on his potential alone. He showed some excellent flashes, but those flashes need to be more of a consistent effort to really reach his potential. Stephen has only received 6 minor penalties in 124 OHL games so far which is extremely impressive for a player who can go into the corners and win battles.

Jonny Brodzinski

Center – St. Cloud State (NCAA)
Born June 19,1993- Coon Rapids, MN
Height 6.00 - Weight 202 - Shoots L

Games	Goals	Assists	Points	PIMS	+/-
42	22	11	33	10	+28

Brodzinski played his first 3 games in the USHL last year where he registered his first point with an assist after being selected 7th overall in the 1st round by Des Moines Buccaneers. He followed it up with a full season playing in 61 games and scoring 33 points including 16 goals, which was the most in the league as a defenseman for the Muskegon Lumberjacks. He possesses great hands to rush the puck up the ice into the offensive zone and he finds lanes to get to the slot to put great shots on net. He is really calm with the puck and he gets his shot through to the net on a fairly consistent basis. He has decent size and skating, moves the puck well on the breakout and can hold on to the puck in the offensive zone to keep the cycle alive. He plays with an element of physicality on the puck carrier. Brodzinski demonstrated this year that he can be effective in the offensive zone but needs to translate that success to his own end moving forward. He needs to make sure he is hard to play against in his own end.

Hunter Garlent

Center – Guelph Storm (OHL)
Born Feb 4, 1995 – St. Catherines, ON
Height 5.08 - Weight 164 - Shoots R

Games	Goals	Assists	Points	PIMS	+/-
50	12	19	31	25	+4

Hunter brings a good level of speed to his game and can beat defenders with a quick outside move. He works hard and always strives to keep his feet moving when he is on the ice, which occasionally earns him the chance to create turnovers from the opposition. Hunter shows flashes of offensive creativity but struggles to bring it consistently night in and night out. Garlent is not afraid to go to the hard areas of the ice to make a play despite his usual size disadvantage to most opponents. He is constantly buzzing around the net and jumps all over rebound opportunities when they become available. He also possesses a rocket of a wrist shot and is able to get it off with a deceptively fast release, fooling goaltenders a number of times top shelf. He shows a lot of intriguing skills but will have to overcome his size and show a little more production offensively to reach his potential. However, he works extremely hard and has shown some real flashes of talent which will work in his favor later on in the draft with a team willing to take a chance on him.

Avery Peterson

Center – Grand Rapids (HS USA)
Born June 20, 95 – Grand Rapids, MN
Height 6.02 - Weight 194 - Shoots L

HOCKEYPROSPECT.COM

DRAFT GUIDE' 13

Games	Goals	Assists	Points	PIMS	+/-
23	23	31	54	2	+3

Peterson played primarily for Grand Rapids High School with a brief 8 game appearance in the USHL with the Sioux City Musketeers joining the team pretty late into the season. He possesses some nice quick hands and drives the puck wide really well into the offensive zone. He put low shots on net to try and generate rebounds for teammates driving the net.

Quotable: "Skating is an issue here. He's hunched over and I don't see much agility. I like his hands but I'm not sure he thinks the game as quickly as I'd like to see. He stayed on the outside and didn't look creative. I probably sound overly negative, but I guess I was just hoping for a lot more because I had heard some talk about him as a possible 2nd rounder. "– Mark Edwards

Martin Reway

LW – Gatineau, Olympics (QMJHL)
Born Jan 24, 1995 – Prague, Czech
Height 5.08 - Weight 158 - Shoots L

HOCKEYPROSPECT.COM

DRAFT GUIDE' 13

Games	Goals	Assists	Points	PIMS	+/-
47	22	28	50	56	-1

His biggest asset is his passing skills and vision. He seems to have eyes all over his head and seems to know where his teammates are at all times on the ice. A dynamic and creative puck-handler, he has quick hands and is able to find space where there doesn't seem to be any. He loves to use his offensive skills to create fancy plays, cross-ice passes, behind the back feeds and risky but spectacular plays. He plays an attractive brand of hockey and you have to live with the downside of some of it. A great powerplay player, he controls the play with ease and shows tremendous poise with the puck before executing a superb pass or getting space for a shot on goal. With the vision he possesses, Reway also has a great sense of anticipation and will takeaway plays by using good positioning or a well placed stick. Physicality will always be an issue for Reway, with such a small frame it is difficult for him to win 1-on-1 battles effectively and will always take physical abuse from bigger players. He didn't show the will to take ahit and rarely initiated a contact in our viewings. His vision and smarts help him a lot in his defensive zone, he understands the fundamentals of positioning, but was sometimes seen cheating in neutral zone while his team didn't retrieve the puck.

Tyler Motte

Center – USNTDP (USHL)
Born March 10, 1995 – St. Clair, MI
Height 5.09 - Weight 190 - Shoots L

Games	Goals	Assists	Points	PIMS	+/-
57	21	16	37	40	+14

Tyler is a shifty two-way forward who can do a lot of things for a hockey team. His skating is outstanding, with fantastic acceleration and agility. He tends to be the first player in on the forecheck and doesn't neglect his own zone either, using great wheels to get back and help his defense. His penalty killing is excellent with sound positioning and a good work ethic, and he's a threat to score shorthanded. He plays physical and doesn't shy away from contact but is limited by his size and sometimes when throwing a hit ends up getting the worst of it. He can make plays with the puck on the rush but at times has trouble creating in the offensive zone. His lack of strength can be a factor against bigger players and he can be shut down completely. Consistency is a major concern, as he can disappear for periods or games at a time. He also appears to have a short fuse and was an easy target for pesky opponents who like to agitate opponents. As detailed, his size is the biggest concern.

Evan Allen

Center – USNTDP (USHL)
Born Feb 3, 1995 – Sterling Heights
Height 5.10 - Weight 190 - Shoots L

Games	Goals	Assists	Points	PIMS	+/-
57	19	24	43	18	+2

There were times this season when the NTDP power play consisted of repeatedly feeding Allen passes for one-timers, to the extent that teammates were forcing pucks through traffic trying to get him the shot. He can absolutely rifle it and is a threat to score from anywhere in the offensive zone, though he's more of a close-your-eyes-and-shoot type than a guy who picks his spots. He also made a positive impression with his work ethic this season, showing on numerous occasions that he's willing to do the little things to win hockey games. He forechecks, back checks, and shows good situational and positional awareness. On the downside, he's really a complementary player and projects as such in the future as well. Though from time to time he shows good jump, his skating is average. What really holds him back is his lack of puck handling ability. Evan on many occasions over the last two years looked like New Jersey prospect Reid Boucher with his tremendous shot coupled with lack of consistency.

Connor Light

Defense – Andover (HS USA)
Born Feb 8, 1995 – Andover, MA
Height 6.05 - Weight 198 - Shoots L

HOCKEYPROSPECT.COM

Games	Goals	Assists	Points	PIMS	+/-
25	6	5	11	36	N/A

Connor possesses an excellent frame and shows some positive attributes on the ice, but is still very raw. His defensive zone positioning is strong and he plays well in front of his net, but has occasional lapses of over aggressiveness. Against the rush, he's hard to beat with good feet and long reach. He can line guys up for big hits along the boards and pinches like a freight train to make plays. His skating is strong and smooth, especially for his size, and does well to skate the puck out of danger and up ice. He shows OK puck skills but his offensive upside is a question mark as his decision-making on the attack is poor at times. Even if his game doesn't completely round out, he's still an intriguing prospect with his combination of size, skating, and physical play. The Omaha Lancers drafted him in the 2013 USHL Draft, and without a college commitment he looks a safe bet to suit up for them in the fall.

Jean-Sebastien Dea

Center – Rouyn Noranda (QMJHL)
Born Feb 8, 1994 – Montreal, PQ
Height 6.00 - Weight 155 - Shoots R

HOCKEYPROSPECT.COM

Games	Goals	Assists	Points	PIMS	+/-
68	45	40	85	59	+21

Dea is a very smart centerman who knows how to make himself available for teammates. He has great offensive execution and his finishing touch is just tremendous. He scored numerous goals on the powerplay and around the net. He anticipates where the play is headed before his teammates executes his play, which is a sign of his great hockey sense. He has an accurate wrist shot that can be released quickly on the rush or on a one-timer. Dea doesn't have great high end speed, dazzling skills or amazing passing skills; but, he has an above-average skills set of all those named attributes. He wins numerous faceoffs and again uses great smarts in his own zone to support his defensemen. His positioning without the puck is great and he will use an active stick to block the passing lanes. We think Dea's high number of points this season is partially due to the fact he was playing with a tremendous passer in Sven Andrighetto. He was also lined with a great overager Gabriel Desjardins. His level of competitiveness in his one-on-one battles is not consistent and he can start gliding at times. Not a physical player, Dea is also a slight stature player and should fill in that frame completely before playing in pro hockey.

Will Toffey

Defense – Salisbury Prep (HS USA)
Born N/A – N/A
Height N/A - Weight N/A - Shoots L

Games	Goals	Assists	Points	PIMS	+/-
N/A	N/A	N/A	N/A	N/A	N/A

Will brings an excellent two-way skillset with top-end skating and shows flashes of gamebreaking ability. He can absolute fly up the ice and is comfortable with the puck at high speed, able to navigate neutral zone traffic and make plays. Though he's overzealous at times with his end-to-end efforts, it's encouraging to see him consistently try to make things happen and he recovers well when he does overcommit himself. He frequently pinches into the attack and can play like a forward with good positioning along the boards. On the powerplay, he can act as quarterback and shows good puck distribution and low shots from the point. He's difficult to beat on the rush with intelligent gap control and good reads, with patience and aggression at the right times. He has the tools to defend well in his zone and generally does so, showing pinpoint footwork, an active stick, and good physical play, but has occasional shifts where he's too lax or chases the play. If he can remove the sporadic gaffes from his game, Toffey has excellent upside.

Spenser Jensen

Defense – Medicine Hat(WHL)
Born July 2, 1995 – Calgary, AB
Height 6.04 - Weight 1191 - Shoots R

Games	Goals	Assists	Points	PIMS	+/-
68	1	9	10	66	-10

Jensen is a defensive defenseman who provides a strong, physical presence from the backend. His game is mostly depended on his work ethic and being a tough player to play against in the defensive zone. Jensen is an average skater, and will be something that he has to improve on for the future. Jensen is not an enforcer, but he will get into scrums and protect his teammates when necessary. He likes to use his body to land big hits along the boards and to be hard to play against in the slot. He is not afraid to block shots, and is more than willing to stand in front of shots to help his goaltender out. His best asset is his stick, as he does a very good job of creating takeaways and protecting the slot. He stirs opponents to the outside quite well, with his stick, but needs to give quicker opponents a larger gap off the rush to not get beat to the net. Jensen is very limited with the puck. His outlet passes need some work as they are not always easy and accurate for his teammates to receive them.

2

PLAYER INTERVIEW

Josh Morrissey

Michelle Sturino speaks to Josh Morrissey of the Prince Albert Raiders

MS: You obviously had a very good rookie season with Prince Albert with 10 goals 38 points in 68 games. Your team wasn't the greatest last season, but do you think you would have been able to get as accustomed as quickly to the WHL if you were on a better team.

JM: It was a tough year for us as a group, obviously with the way things ended up finishing at the end of the season. As a team we weren't where we wanted to be. Individually I was able to be given an opportunity to play. I learned a lot of lessons, some of them I think you wouldn't have wanted to learn necessarily. They were tough in losing and how not to let that mentality set into your game. I think you know statistic wise as a team, we didn't achieve anything close to what we wanted to. A lot of lessons for myself where I could learn and take forward with me into this season and the offseason last summer. It was obviously a tough year, I was thankful to be given the opportunities that I was given. Obviously in a tough situation like that I was given more chances than in a situation where you have a pretty veteran D. We had a lot of young guys so I was able to step in and play a lot. I really have to thank the coaching staff for giving me the opportunity and like I said it was a tough year but we could build on a lot of things.

MS: You played on a very talented Team Canada that won Gold at the Ivan Hlinka Tournament over the summer. You played against a lot of the same players that were on that team in the Top

Prospects Game in January. What is the biggest difference in your game from the Summer to now.

JM: I've been trying to work on all aspects of my game really. You hear about guys like Sidney Crosby and others who talk about it all the time, trying to add new elements to their game, different skills. Trying to get better at everything all the time. I think if you watch me now I have a few extra elements in my game. I've been trying to work on my shot a lot, creativity with the puck in the offensive zone. Obviously now with the NHL back being able to watch guys like Erik Karlsson and Kris Letang. Fortunately there's a lot of those good defensemen out there that you're able to watch. From watching guys like that I think you can pick up things, watching a lot of video with our coaching staff, Dave Manson. I guess maybe there's not one particular thing that might be a big difference from the summer. But I think as a whole I've added some little skills and things to it that I may not have had from the summer.

MS: You mentioned your shot, it's very accurate. What have you been working on perhaps power? I also know you got to speak with Mike Green over the summer, what was he telling you?

JM: Yeah, that's an amazing luxury I have when I train at Crashed Conditioning in Calgary to see NHL players and pro working right there next to you and how hard they work. But also pick their brains at times. Obviously you don't want to be too annoying I guess you could say, but when you do talk to them, you know Greener as a defenseman and an offensive guy, he had a lot of good tips. One specifically was I think a lot of times tries try to make the perfect shot, or get everything you can get into it, a lot of power. But once you get to the next level, goalies are just so quick that it's often you don't have a lot of time and space so it's that quick release or one-timer or it's on your stick then off your stick you could fool goalies or beat them because they're so quick and technically strong now. I think individually a lot of times I look to make a pass first in the offensive zone, I like the backdoor plays on the power play. Something I've been working on lately is shooting the puck more, and using my shot, shooting through screens. Whether it's on the side on the power play or the top or 5 on 5, shooting through screens or moving the puck a couple inches trying to get a better shooting angle. Just some little skills that obviously takes time to develop, but I think I've been having some success with lately.

MS: Absolutely, and once you basically show teams you're a threat and that you can take that shot, it obviously opens teams up for your teammates right?

JM: For sure, I think that's something that, like I mentioned I'm always trying to work on and coaches are on me for is shooting the puck. I think we have success when I do, like you said it opens up other options and sometimes it fortunately goes in as well.

MS: Your stats have shown you can be a bit of a streaky scorer from time to time with a lot of multi point games this season, and stretches where you're not on the score sheet. Now is that due to a whole team performance, or does this worry you at all considering your style of play.

JM: I don't think it worries me too much, I think it's just the way it goes. I think as a player, individually as long as the teams having success whether you're putting up points or not, obviously you're happy and I think being an offensive or two-way style defenseman I would like to put up points all the time, who wouldn't. But I think at times you just get unfortunate or unlucky and sometimes those games where maybe you're not getting points as frequently are sometimes your best games as opposed to some nights where you don't play what you think is your best game and wind up with 2 or 3 points. So I think it's been interesting for me this year, I think I've had some chances where I've been kinda snakebitten some unlucky times, but at the same time as long as I think I'm doing the right things in those games and putting myself in the position to get pucks on the back door, making lanes, and shooting. I try not to put too much pressure on myself then because atleast I'm doing the right things and getting the chances. So I guess it's kinda interesting the streaks, but as long as the team is doing well it's alright.

MS: Before the season started you said your goal was to be a 60 to 70 point player. So far you've pretty much equaled your point totals from last year. What kind of road bumps have you encountered that maybe slowed you down a little bit from reaching that potential goal.

JM: I guess as a defenseman our power play hasn't been clicking as well as we've wanted it to be this year. Obviously being a power play guy, that's where maybe I could have got some points from. But at the start of the year I wasn't putting much onus on the fact I wanted to be a 60 or 70 point guy. More so on the fact I wanna be that guy to create those chances and I guess be a threat when I'm on the ice that the other team has to worry about. I definitely want to be higher statistic wise than I am right now. But at the same time I've gotten unlucky at times and sometimes that's just the way it goes. Like I said I'm not too worried about it I think as long as I'm doing the right things in my game and the points will come. If they're not coming, that's why we have video and continue to watch and see where I can create more chances, so I'm not too worried about it I guess.

3

2013
NHL DRAFT PROSPECTS

Sam Reinhart

Center – Kootenay Ice
Born Nov 6, 1995 – Vancouver, BC
Height 6.00 - Weight 182 - Shoots R

HOCKEYPROSPECT.COM

DRAFT GUIDE '13

Games	Goals	Assists	Points	PIMS	+/-
72	35	50	85	22	+8

In his second season, Sam Reinhart has continued to dominate games offensively despite the lack of help he gets from his teammates. Opposing teams clearly target him and have game plans around him as he is really the only legitimate threat to do any damage for Kootenay, and yet Reinhart has been able to get through it and produce offensively.

Like last season, Reinhart had a bit of a slow start to the year offensively, but really picked up his play as the season went along. His playmaking abilities are already one of the best in the league, and opponents really have a difficult time trying to contain him and take away his time and space. He is able to create chance after chance around the net no matter what kind of pressure he receives. He is very fast on his skates, and opponents have a difficult time trying to pin him up along the walls because he is so strong and quick on his feet to spin away from hits. Reinhart seems to have eyes located in the back of his head, as he makes unbelievable behind the back passes, tape to tape. Reinhart could shoot the puck more as he has good stick-handling abilities and a good release to his shots, but you cannot question his decisions to pass when they seem to always accomplish something.

Reinhart's play has improved without the puck this season. He has shown more intensity along the walls to win battles for pucks and to get the attack going again. He is not afraid to block shots, but he could block them more often from a game to game basis. He plays so much on the PP and on even strength that he does not receive much PK minutes, but he could probably do an admirable job as his ability to read the play is good, and he possesses a pretty good stick as well.

There is no question that Reinhart will be a top end pick if he can continue to put up the numbers that he has in the last two seasons. He desperately needs some help in order to help his team win as he cannot be out on the ice every second of the game, but he has been able to make some average players look quite good this season, which is really the ultimate compliment for any player. He comes from a hockey family who will undoubtedly provide good advice to get through any difficult times he may face as a player and as the captain of the Kootenay Ice next season, which is always a positive for any player.

William Nylander

Center – Sodertalje
Born May 1, 1996 – Calgary, AB
Height 5,10 - Weight 170 - Shoots R

HOCKEYPROSPECT.COM

DRAFT GUIDE' 13

Games	Goals	Assists	Points	PIMS	+/-
8	4	2	6	2	+2

William, the son of former NHLer Michael Nylander, is an extremely talented and dynamic forward who spent last season between Sodertalje's J20 team and their men's team playing in the Allsvenskan league. In J20 he put up nearly two points per game and in the men's league, nearly a point per game as a 17 year old.

William may in fact be the most absolute dynamic, creative and flashy player you will find in the 2014 NHL Entry Draft. He has exceptional puck skills and can create highlight reel goals on any given shift. He has quick hands and is extremely difficult to contain. He combines this with his skating ability which sports a quick acceleration allowing him to hit top speed very quickly. To top it all off he has an absolute laser of a shot which he can let fly quickly and at a high speed. He has a wealth of natural talent and he has shown clear signs of high level vision and hockey sense making him dangerous every time he steps on the ice.

William is not without his flaws however. He can sometimes forget he has teammates and try to take on the other team by himself. These plays showed the flashes of his skill but usually wound up unsuccessful and heading in the opposite direction. When the play does go in the opposite direction, Nylander tends to lack the urgency to get back and defend. Of course at his size, we would like to see him get stronger. He fends off checks fairly well, but he will only become that much better by adding muscle.

Quotable: "I remember the first time I ever saw William play. My first reaction was "wow" because of his skill level. He's a player that actually frustrates me at times because he has the potential to not just be good, but the potential to be a really special player. I hope he realizes that he only hurts himself when trying to take on the entire team by himself, because when he shows his skating and hands while playing within a system, it's an amazing sight to see." – Ryan Yessie

Aaron Ekblad

Defense– Barrie Colts
Born Feb 7, 1996 – Belle River,ON
Height 6.04 - Weight 213 - Shoots R

Games	Goals	Assists	Points	PIMS	+/-
54	7	27	34	64	+29

Despite Ekblad was selected 1st overall in the 2011 OHL entry draft after he was the second player ever (after John Tavares) to receive exceptional player status drafted a year ahead of other players his age. Aaron was selected out of the Sun County Panthers organization following in his brother's footsteps who was selected by the London Knights in 2009.

Ekblad possesses excellent size and entered the league at the age of 15 scoring 10 goals and 29 points in his rookie season, which he followed up with 34 points this year and a +29 rating. He moves up and down the ice effectively but his skating style is rather sloppy. He displays his strength in battles along the walls and infront of his own net. He has been hit or miss one on one, when successful he displays strength and uses his size to edge players out and keep them from gaining the inside track to the net. He can distribute the puck effectively in the offensive zone to create scoring chances and has an excellent shot from the point. Aaron generally looks his best when he's in the offensive zone. Despite his size and the hype he has behind him, he has struggled defensively in our viewings and his reaction time isn't what we'd hope and his positioning is not always idea. He has gained a ton of experience which should only help him.

He's expected to be a high pick in the 2014 NHL Entry Draft, but simply needs to clean up his skating and become more consistent in the defensive zone. We've seen a lot of bright spots and a high ceiling in his potential, but there is clearly still work to be done for Ekblad.

Quotable: "I take back what I said earlier, he was not good today." - NHL Scout

Quotable: "I thought he had a few rough shifts at the U17 but logged a lot of minutes and followed up the tourney with a strong run towards the playoffs. Had some great games in the playoffs and some average ones. The potential is obviously off the charts." - Mark Edwards

Roland McKeown

Defense – Kingston Frontenacs
Born Jan 20, 1996 – Listowel, ON
Height 6.01 - Weight 186 - Shoots R

HOCKEYPROSPECT.COM

DRAFT GUIDE '13

Games	Goals	Assists	Points	PIMS	+/-
61	7	22	29	33	-24

Toronto Marlboros Minor Midget program. Roland came into the OHL Draft as the undisputed top defensive prospect and was able to show why as he made a near seamless transition to the OHL as a 16 year old.

Roland plays an excellent two-way game. He has great combination of size and skating ability. He rushes the puck up ice extremely well and shows fluid ability to evade checkers and acquire the offensive zone. He possesses a strong shot from the point and is an effective puck mover in all three zones identifying passing lanes very quickly in the offensive zone. He is also capable of making a smart play up ice hitting teammates in stride. Thanks to his skating and size Roland is pretty effective regularly in one on one match-up's and when his team is pinned deep he shows good positioning. Roland is a player we'd like to see develop a little more of a mean streak. He will finish his hits but we'd like to see him play with a little more aggression than he does right now. He leads a little more towards the offensive side of the game, but has shown he can be reliable defensively. We'd like to see more of that as he has one season under his belt. We would also like to see more consistency. Roland didn't play to his capabilities in a couple of our viewings this season.

The sky is the limit for McKeown who looks to show he is one of the best defensemen available in the 2014 NHL Entry Draft.

Quotable: "Ever since I saw Roland play up with the Toronto Marlboros Minor Midget team a year before his OHL Draft year I've been excited to see what he would do at this level. He's extremely complete and smart. I received mixed viewings of him but I remain confident that McKeown will be a player who ends up close to the top of the draft board at the 2014 NHL Entry Draft. There's so much to like about him and he's in a great situation in Kingston." – Ryan Yessie

Jared McCann

Center – Soo Greyhounds
Born May 31, 1996 – London, ON
Height 6.00 - Weight 174 - Shoots L

Games	Goals	Assists	Points	PIMS	+/-
64	41	23	44	35	-6

Jared was highly regarded by HockeyProspect and was ranked #2 behind only Connor McDavid in our 2012 OHL Draft Guide. He was eventually selected 4th Overall by the Sault Ste. Marie Greyhounds at the 2012 OHL Priority Selection Draft.

McCann had an outstanding rookie season for the Greyhounds. He immediately jumped right into the Greyhounds line up and needed a little time to find his groove, but when he did he was a consistently effective player splitting time between the second and third lines. Jared finished his final 9 games of the season posting 16 points in 9 games played. He brings a number of offensive skills to the table and possesses a quick burst of speed when cutting through the middle of the ice that catches many defenders flat footed. Jared displays excellent vision and is particularly so successful because of his very high level of hockey sense. He reads the game at a level higher than most of his peers and it allows him to create, execute and read plays that some players simply cannot. He scored a number of highlight reel goals this season and possesses an absolute rocket of a wrist shot with a lightning quick release that catches many goaltenders off guard.

McCann was very physical in midget and we expect he will bring even more of that side of his game in the OHL. He was not afraid of corners or battles in front of the net against bigger opponents. He is also very reliable in the defensive zone and is more aware than many rookies at helping out defenders down low and moving pucks up ice quickly. He is strong in the face-off circle and wins the majority of draws he takes. Jared provided good scoring depth on the second power play lineup for the Greyhounds displaying good offensive awareness and playmaking abilities. He shows creative one on one moves when skating with the puck. Jared missed time in the playoffs due to concussion reasons but should be ready to go by the start of next season.

McCann will be looking to improve on an impressive rookie season by not only being one of the main contributors in the Greyhounds arsenal but will also expect to hear his name called very early in the 2014 NHL Draft.

Leon Draisaitl

Center – Prince Albert Raiders
Born Oct 27, 1995 – Cologne, GER
Height 6.01 - Weight 198 - Shoots L

HOCKEYPROSPECT.COM

DRAFT GUIDE' 13

Games	Goals	Assists	Points	PIMS	+/-
64	21	37	58	22	+22

Draisaitl has unbelievable vision out on the ice, uses his body well to protect the puck along the walls and then feeds his teammates with excellent passes when they get open for good scoring chances. As a rookie, Draisaitl has received a lot of attention from opposing teams, but he has consistently been able to produce points regardless of the amount of pressure he faced.

The best asset of Draisaitl is definitely he playmaking ability. He can thread a pass cross ice with a perfect saucer pass, make a one touch pass to an open player in the slot or make a behind the pass to a streaking teammate down the middle. Draisaitl is very unpredictable, and seems to always be able to find a play out on the ice that generates some sort of a chance for the Raiders. Not many players at his age can make the types of plays he can with the puck, and he seems to read the play a step ahead of everybody else. In terms of goal scoring ability, Draisaitl is definitely a pass first player, but he has shown the ability to finish in tight and quickly releasing the puck around the slot when given the opportunity. He has very good stickhandling abilities and is able to deke by opponents and use his long reach to his advantage.

An area of improvement for Draisaitl would be his skating abilities. He needs to work on his acceleration and overall speed. He covers a lot of ground with his long strides, but he could be quicker out on the ice to provide another weapon in his game. Defensively, Draisaitl is not bad in his own end. His ability to read the play without the puck improved, and looked like he was adjusting to the physical game of the league well. He could do a better job of being a more physical player and hit opponents off the puck.

Draisaitl's potential is through the roof with his playmaking abilities. His play in his own end will improve with more experience and coaching as he continues to log minutes.

Nikolay Goldobin

Left Wing –Sarnia Sting
Born Oct 7, 1995 - Russia
Height 5.11 - Weight 165 - Shoots L

Games	Goals	Assists	Points	PIMS	+/-
68	30	38	68	12	-7

Goldobin was selected high in two drafts this past summer. Metallurg Novokuznetsk of the KHL selected Nikolay 8th Overall and Sarnia Sting selected him 36th Overall in the CHL Import Draft.

Nikolay was a little apprehensive to open the season. You could see his talent but he just didn't apply himself. Every game he played, Nikolay noticeably improved. His strongest asset is his vision. Goldobin sees the ice so well and uses this ability to make absolutely perfect passes through traffic. He makes difficult passes look easy and hits low percentage passes on a regular basis. He's extremely creative and has excellent hands. He was very good on the breakway including shootouts thanks to his hands and quick release but it was his passing that brought fans out of their seats and got scouts talking. We would like to see Nikolay get an extra gear in his skating. While he moves well he doesn't really have that breakout speed that would make him that much better.

He definitely needs to get stronger and be more willing to take physicality. All season he looked a little timid in the neutral zone and would poke at pucks but wouldn't risk getting hit hard in netural ice to make a play and he needs to be more willing to take physicality and hopefully get stronger to more comfortably handle this side of the game. Nikolay has the potential to be the top forward selected out of the OHL at the 2014 NHL Entry Draft.

Quotable: "As a resident of Sarnia, I got to make a short 5km trip to the RBC Centre to watch Nikolay develop in plenty of games this season. His hands are special and he looks like he has ice in his veins when he controls the puck in the offensive zone. His vision is exceptional. I just need to see him work harder in the neutral and defensive zones. He looks timid around physical engagement, and that's the only thing that could keep him out of the top 10 at this point. There were actually several games this season where I actually liked Nikolay more than I did Nail Yakupov in some of his games as an OHL rookie. He doesn't have the breakout speed Nail does, but his vision and the way he reads the play may already be better." – Ryan Yessie

Sam Bennett

Center – Kingston Frontenacs
Born June 20, 1996- Holland landing
Height 6.00 - Weight 168 - Shoots L

Games	Goals	Assists	Points	PIMS	+/-
60	18	22	40	87	-2

Sam was selected 9th Overall by the Kingston Frontenacs at the 2012 OHL Priority Selection Draft out of the Toronto Marlboros Minor Midget program. Bennett really seemed to grow as his Minor Midget season went on and was one of the most improved players over the course of that season.

Sam immediately joined the Frontenacs and became a regular player in the top six forwards playing every game situation especially power plays. Sam creates plays extremely well and is able to beat defensemen one on one. He's able to draw in opponents with puck possession and utilizes strong vision to complete difficult pass and create scoring chances. Sam has a pretty strong shot and isn't shy about utilizing it. Sam is a very offensive minded player who is most successful making plays happen, but is also an effective forechecker, can force turnovers.

Sam will need to try and limit the number of minor penalties he takes. 87 penalty minutes is ok if you're dropping the gloves, but with only one fight, that's simply too many minor penalties for a player of his talent to take. Sam will once again be a big time contributor to the Kingston Frontenacs who are on the way up.

Quotable: "I remember seeing him with the Marlboros early on in Minor Midget thinking Sam would be a great sleeper. But when he broke out a couple months into the season that theory went out the window and his upside was no longer a secret. Sam has really benefitted from his hard work. First turning himself into a top 10 pick in Minor Midget, then playing big minutes in Kingston. The Frontenacs made a great pick and are letting him play. I love his instincts and ability to create plays consistently in the offensive zone. I plan on making several trips up to Kingston this coming season and Sam is a big reason for that." – Ryan Yessie

Michael Dal Colle

Left Wing– Oshawa Generals
Born June 20,1996 – Vaughan, ON
Height 6.02 - Weight 171 - Shoots L

Games	Goals	Assists	Points	PIMS	+/-
63	15	33	48	18	+19

Michael was selected 1st Round, 7th Overall by the Oshawa Generals out of the Vaughan Kings Minor Midget program. Michael was one of the premier forwards in all of Ontario leading into the draft. He played ridiculous minutes with Vaughan, so we knew going in he would be well conditioned to play big ice in the OHL.

Early on he established himself showing his potential and winding up on a line with Columbus Blue Jackets' prospect Boone Jenner and Toronto Maple Leafs Tyler Biggs. They maintained this line for the vast majority of this season. Michael is an excellent playmaker and shows creativity with the puck well beyond his years. He visualizes plays well and has a high percentage of success rate on his passing, even in difficult situations. His effort is consistent and he is able to create several scoring chances over the course of a game. Despite his size he's a pretty good skater with efficient quickness. Michael already plays a mature, well rounded game and we hope for him to gain more strength and become a little more physical with his game. Michael is one of the top prospects for the 2014 NHL Entry Draft and will be one of the go to guys for the Generals next season.

Quotable: "We don't have the numbers, but I would be surprised if there was a forward in Minor Midget that played as much as Dal Colle did in his OHL Draft Year. It sure prepared him for his rookie season with Oshawa. He's so mature and creative on the ice, it made him a great fit with Jenner and Biiggs. Michael in my mind is one of the premier playmakers in the 2014 NHL Entry Draft. I hope he's working on his cardio this summer because his ice time is only going to increase in Oshawa next year. I just want more consistency from him." – Ryan Yessie

Nicholas Ritchie

LW – Peterborough Petes
Born Dec 5, 1995 - Orangeville, ON
Height 6.02 - Weight 218 - Shoots L

Games	Goals	Assists	Points	PIMS	+/-
41	18	17	35	50	-10

Nick was selected first round, 2nd overall by the Peterborough Petes at the 2011 OHL Priority Selection Draft out of the Toronto Marlboros Minor Midget program.

Nick made an immediate impact in the OHL still at the age of 15 due to his late birthdate. Nick had an impressive rookie season including a brief but successful performance at the World U17 Challenge in Windsor. Nick entered the 2012-2013 season unable to enter his NHL Draft year due to his birth date. This turned out to be a positive as Ritchie had multiople issues with his shoulder this season and was limited to 41 games. Nick is a big power forward. When he's on his game he plays with a great deal of energy, finishes his checks hard and he can be very dangerous in the offensive zone. He has good offensive skills, handles the puck well and gets off a powerful shot. He is a very shoot first type of player who is capable of putting the puck in the net. Unfortunately he struggles with consistency and can be invisible, or even a liability when he is not on his game.

Nick has the potential to be a top 5 pick in the 2014 NHL Entry Draft, however needs to become much more consistent and show how dangerous he can be on a nightly basis. The Petes are on the rise, and Nick will need to be one of their leaders.

Quotable: "Depending on what night you see Nick play, he's debatably the best player in the entire 2014 NHL Draft class, or he's not even a first round. There seems to be no middle ground on my viewings. Every time I saw Peterborough this year he was either outstanding, invisible, or injured. There's a world of upside in Ritchie, but next year is his third OHL season and I want to see more consistency in his game. Nick could be a big mover one way or the other on our draft board next season." – Ryan Yessie

Brycen Martin

Defense – Swift Current
Born May 9, 1996 – Calgary, AB
Height 6.01 - Weight 181 - Shoots L

Games	Goals	Assists	Points	PIMS	+/-
67	2	17	19	32	+3

Martin is a poised, puck moving defenseman who really impressed scouts this season with his play with the puck this year. He looked like he was a veteran in the league, and played with confidence that is rarely seen in players at his age in the WHL.

It is fun to watch Martin move the puck and calmly skate out of trouble and buy some more time for himself to make a pass to his teammates. He is always looking to make a play with the puck, and will only go glass and out when his team is in real trouble defensively and they need to eliminate the pressure that they face. Martin is already quarterbacking the PP for the Broncos, and did a very good job of distributing pucks from the blue line. He may not have picked up many points this season, but he displayed above average vision from the point. He needs to work on his shots and using it more often from the point.

Defensively, Martin's game still has some improvements to make. He needs to do a better job of angling opponents along the boards, and not allowing them to get by him. His work with his stick can be improved, as he was not able to knock away passes and shots on a consistent basis. He was out of the shooting lane often to allow his goaltender to take the shot, but did sacrifice his body to block shots once in a while. He could be a little more physical along the walls, and will definitely have to fill out his frame for the future.

Martin will definitely be receiving more ice time and be counted on to provide a more defensive presence next season. He will have to show that he is not a liability out on the ice against the offensively skilled players on a consistent basis, and be tougher to play against. Martin will have adjusted his game to the WHL level, and he will definitely increase his points total and improve his puck moving abilities as the season goes on, which will attract the attention of NHL teams.

Quotable: "His first game at the U17 was fantastic, he looked to tire a bit later in the tourney as he made some mental mistakes. Overall, he made a good impression." - Mark Edwards

Jake Virtanen

LW – Calgary Hitmen
Born Aug 17, 1996 – Abbotsford, BC
Height 6.01 - Weight 190 - Shoots R

Games	Goals	Assists	Points	PIMS	+/-
62	16	18	34	67	+25

Jake Virtanen is a physical power forward who is quick to get around the ice and possesses very good offensive skills. When he is at his best, opponents have a tough time stopping him from getting to the net and creating havoc. The issue with Virtanen's game is his inconsistency. He has too many games where he is invisible, and makes very little impact out on the ice. He has all the tools to be a high, first round draft pick in 2014, but he has to be able to put it all together on a consistent basis.

Virtanen is very good at getting to the net with his strength and speed, when he wants to. He does not use his body nearly enough to his advantage to create more scoring chances. He possesses good hands and likes to dangle off the rush, but he also needs to dump and chase more often to limit the turnovers that he commits. When he gets in on the forecheck, he has the ability to create a lot of turnovers and make life miserable for opponents. Virtanen also loves to shoot from everywhere, which is something he will need to work on and use his teammates more often in the offensive zone. His ability to think the game does not seem to be at a high level, which may be a concern for the future.

Defensively, Virtanen has some work to do in his own end. He uses his body effectively to land big hits out in the neutral zone and along the boards, but he needs to be better at containing opponents and limiting the plays that they have with the puck, especially at the higher level as players will be much smarter and quicker.

It will be interesting to see the role that Virtanen will receive with Calgary next season, and how he will respond to the added responsibility. He will surely have to produce much more offense than he did this season for the Hitmen to have a successful year, and it may be what Virtanen needed to be a more consistent player. If he can be a dangerous player every game, he will definitely be a first round pick.

Ivan Barbashev

LW – Moncton Wildcats
Born Dec 14, 1995 – Moscow, RUS
Height 6.01 - Weight 185 - Shoots L

HOCKEYPROSPECT.COM

DRAFT GUIDE' 13

Games	Goals	Assists	Points	PIMS	+/-
68	18	44	62	36	+9

Barbashev has a complete package of speed, skills and physical abilities. He is a very gifted skater with a good burst of speed that allows him to carry the puck all over the ice and make aggressive approaches in the offensive zone. He likes to use his body to beat the defenders when entering the offensive zone. He also uses his quick hands to elude players and has shown very good puck skills thus far. He is dynamic with his very strong hands and he also takes dangerous shots on goal. He has also displayed his great offensive hockey sense, distributing the puck and creating superb plays around the net for teammates. Barbashev is a threat every time he touches the puck but he also plays a strong game without it. He is an intense player and we like his hustle on the ice. He takes a liking to finishing his checks and showed he can deliver some very hard ones. He is hard working and will rarely take a night off, showing heart and desire in his defensive zone. He is willing to battle through traffic to create plays and crash the opposition's crease.

Nikita Lyamkin

Defense – Kuznetskie -Medbedi
Born Feb 6, 1996 – Russia
Height 6.03 - Weight 165 - Shoots L

HOCKEYPROSPECT.COM

DRAFT GUIDE' 13

Games	Goals	Assists	Points	PIMS	+/-
13	0	0	0	8	-3

Nikita spent the past season in the MHL and enjoyed very successful World U-17 Challenge in Victoriaville/Drummondville, helping Russia to a Silver Medal. Nikita has excellent size and displays an exceptional level of hockey sense. He is extremely strong positionally and always seems to be in the right place on the ice. He is a strong skater with good mobility allowing him to match up against forwards very well one on one. He rarely if ever gets beat. Nikita shows a willingness to battle along the wall with a nastiness in his game. He won the majority of battles, he will win even more as he gets stronger within his big frame. Nikita isn't PK Subban rushing the puck but he did display the ability to lug it up ice and gain the zone. He makes a very smart first pass and makes quick decisions in all three zones with the puck. He also possesses a good point shot. There is very little negatives in Nikita's game, we were extremely impressed with him in our viewings. He definitely needs to get stronger before he can start realizing his true potential. He has the size but not the strength.

Blake Clarke

LW – Brampton Battalion
Born Jan 24, 1996 – Wildwood, MO
Height 6.01 - Weight 190 - Shoots L

Games	Goals	Assists	Points	PIMS	+/-
68	19	32	51	42	-2

Blake was selected first round, 15th Overall at the 2012 OHL Priority Selection Draft by the Brampton Battalion out of the St. Louis Blues U18 program. Clarke also split the season with the Fargo Force of the USHL as a 15 year old. Blake Clarke came on in a big way for the traditionally offensively starved Brampton Battalion. He was thrust into key offensive situations as a top 6 forward and top powerplay player and performed well. He has a great combination of skating ability, hands, and creativity in the offensive end. Moreover, in viewings, he did not look out of place in the defensive zone. While in some games Clarke was not as noticeable for the full 60 minutes as one would like, you can't deny his rookie season production. If he can put together another strong season, he will have to be mentioned with the likes of the highest tier prospects for the NHL 2014 draft.

Nick Schmaltz

Center – Green Bay Gamblers
Born Feb 23, 1996 – Verona, WI
Height 5.11 - Weight 160 - Shoots R

Games	Goals	Assists	Points	PIMS	+/-
64	18	34	52	15	+2

Nick is one of the top forwards available heading into the 2014 NHL Entry Draft and he proved exactly why in his second season with the USHL's Green Bay Gamblers. Nick first appeared with the Chicago Mission U16 program at the age of just 13 years old. Nick would spend 3 years with them joining Green Bay at the end of his third year. With some of the Gamblers veterans moving on after their Clark Cup championship, Nick was called upon to be one of their offensive leaders. Schmaltz possesses excellent skating ability and he is very elusive moving up the ice with the puck eluding checkers. He shows poise and confidence with the puck and likes to create scoring chances for his linemates. He is much more of a playmaker than a finisher. He has a pretty good shot, and if anything we would like to see him take the shot a little more often. He could stand to add a little more muscle as he heads into his NHL Draft Year next season. Nick was selected in the 4th round of the 2012 OHL Priority Selection Draft by the Windsor Spitfires. Schmaltz is committed to the University of North Dakota.

Oskar Lindblom

RW – Brynas
Born Aug 15th, 1996 – Galva, SWE
Height 6.01 - Weight 192 - Shoots L

HOCKEYPROSPECT.COM

DRAFT GUIDE'13

Games	Goals	Assists	Points	PIMS	+/-
22	20	21	41	4	+40

Oskar is an excellent offensive talent who has primarily only played against players his own age, but has been dominant in his age group. This was very prevalent at the 2013 World U-17 Challenge where he posted 13 points in 6 games. Oskar is much more of a shooter than a passer and displays excellent hands in close and makes plays with the puck in tight areas that few players are able to accomplish. He has the ability to score some highlight reel goals and beat defenders and goaltenders in one on one situations. He doesn't pass a whole lot, but when he does it's generally accurate. His lack of a playmaking presence is primarily due to his preference to shoot the puck rather than an inability to make effective passes. HE really hasn't shown much outside offensive ability and we'd like to see him work hard for the puck and get back defensively more often. He's clearly a gifted offensive player, but what may see him stuck behind others is players with comparable offensive ability who provide another dimension to their game.

Kasperi Kapanen

LW – KalPa
Born July 23, 1996 – Kuoeio,FIN
Height 5.10 - Weight 165 - Shoots R

HOCKEYPROSPECT.COM

DRAFT GUIDE'13

Games	Goals	Assists	Points	PIMS	+/-
13	4	0	4	2	+1

Kasperi is a good skater who is not shy around the physical game. Although he's a player we feel needs to add muscle he's packs an effective check and we've witnessed him delivering some pretty solid checks. He is capable of providing a relentless forecheck and can force turnovers. When he's on his game he displays some creative puck control and can beat defenders one on one. He's particularly dangerous on breakaways and shootouts and can finish regularly when he comes in alone on a goaltender. He has good awareness on the rush showing the ability to pass, but quite often he's much more comfortable shooting the puck, even if it means forcing the shot sometimes. Kasperi has shown well in the defensive zone battling and even blocking shots in penalty killing situations while being a dangerous option should he steal the puck and get a bit of a break on the defensemen. We've seen him play quite a bit this season, and while he's a key factor in a lot of games, there are some where he just simply disappears and is not very visible. We would like to see him clear this up a little bit moving forward as he leads the charge for Finland towards the 2014 NHL Entry Draft.

Anton Karlsson

RW – Frolunda jr 20
Born Aug 3, 1996 – Lerum, SWE
Height 6.01 - Weight 187 - Shoots L

HOCKEYPROSPECT.COM

Games	Goals	Assists	Points	PIMS	+/-
17	4	4	8	4	+6

Anton has very good size for a player his age and plays an aggressive style of play finishing his checks whenever possible. He plays with a great deal of energy and forechecks hard. While he has excellent work ethic and his turnover numbers are impressive, he's not a flashy offensive player and tends to predatorily work his way into primary scoring areas and gets open. He relies on of his very high level hockey sense and vision which helps him see the play faster than his opponents, giving him the jump on the play. While he has a powerful shot, he is an effective passer and makes some slick passes look effortless. Anton battles hard in all three zones and will backcheck hard, taking away time and space from opponents in the offensive zone and clear the zone. On the penalty kill he generally puts a lot of pressure on the point and has shown a willingness to block shots.

Jacob Middleton

Defense – Ottawa 67's (OHL)
Born Jan 2, 1996 – Stratford, ON
Height 6.03 - Weight 194 - Shoots L

HOCKEYPROSPECT.COM

Games	Goals	Assists	Points	PIMS	+/-
29	1	4	5	25	-13

Jacob was selected first round, 8th Overall by the Owen Sound Attack at the 2012 OHL Priority Selection Draft out of the Huron-Perth Lakers Minor Midget program. Jacob joined the Attack but quickly suffered an injury limiting his action in the first half of the season. He returned in time to play a prominent role on the blueline for Team Ontario at the World U-17 Challenge. Jacob then was traded to the Ottawa 67's at the trade deadline. Jacob played big minutes the rest of the way for the 67's and really took over where he left off from the U-17 Challenge providing an excellent two-way presence for Ottawa. Jacob is very solid in one on one situations. He can get beat, but generally keeps a strong gap control and can win the one on one match-up with both his stick and his body. He displays a physical edge at times and finishes his checks hard, although he doesn't possess much of a mean streak. Jacob moves the puck extremely well up ice and can be relied upon to make the smart decision on the point on the power play. He also possesses a pretty strong shot from the point that he can get through the crowd. Middleton is a pretty complete defenseman. He doesn't really have one single standout ability but doesn't have a major flaw in his game either.

4

2013 PLAYER RANKINGS

Rank	CS	PLAYER	Team	League	Pos.	Ht	Wt
1	2	NATHAN MACKINNON	HALIFAX	QMJHL	RC	6' 0"	182
2	1	SETH JONES	PORTLAND	WHL	RD	6' 3.5"	205
3	3	JONATHAN DROUIN	HALIFAX	QMJHL	LW	5' 10.5"	186
4	2	VALERI NICHUSHKIN	CHELYABINSK	RUSSIA	RW	6' 4"	202
5	1	ALEKSANDER BARKOV	TAPPARA	FINLAND	LC	6' 3"	209
6	5	SEAN MONAHAN	OTTAWA	OHL	LC	6' 2.25"	187
7	3	ELIAS LINDHOLM	BRYNAS	SWEDEN	RC	6' 0"	192
8	22	NIKITA ZADOROV	LONDON	OHL	LD	6' 5.25"	221
9	4	RASMUS RISTOLAINEN	TPS	FINLAND	RD	6' 4"	207
10	19	MAX DOMI	LONDON	OHL	C/LW	5' 9.25"	197
11	15	BO HORVAT	LONDON	OHL	LC	6' 0"	206
12	5	ALEXANDER WENNBERG	DJURGARDEN	SWEDEN-2	LC	6' 1"	190
13	7	VALENTIN ZYKOV	BAIE-COMEAU	QMJHL	LW	5' 11.75"	209
14	1	ZACH FUCALE	HALIFAX	QMJHL	G	6' 1"	181
15	32	MADISON BOWEY	KELOWNA	WHL	RD	6' 0.75"	195
16	4	DARNELL NURSE	SOO	OHL	LD	6' 3.5"	185
17	27	JOSHUA MORRISSEY	PRINCE ALBERT	WHL	LD	5' 11.75"	186
18	23	SAMUEL MORIN	RIMOUSKI	QMJHL	LD	6' 6.25"	202
19	10	ANTHONY MANTHA	VAL-D'OR	QMJHL	RW	6' 3.75"	190
20	16	RYAN HARTMAN	PLYMOUTH	OHL	RW	5' 11"	181
21	20	CURTIS LAZAR	EDMONTON	WHL	C/RW	5' 11.75"	190
22	26	ADAM ERNE	QUEBEC	QMJHL	LW	6' 0.5"	210
23	25	MORGAN KLIMCHUK	REGINA	WHL	LW	5' 11.25"	180
24	6	HUNTER SHINKARUK	MEDICINE HAT	WHL	C/LW	5' 10.25"	181
25	33	NICOLAS PETAN	PORTLAND	WHL	LC	5' 8.5"	165
26	14	CHRIS BIGRAS	OWEN SOUND	OHL	LD	6' 0.5"	186
27	39	EMILE POIRIER	GATINEAU	QMJHL	LW	6' 0.75"	183
28	17	KERBY RYCHEL	WINDSOR	OHL	LW	6' 0.75"	205
29	8	FREDERIK GAUTHIER	RIMOUSKI	QMJHL	LC	6' 4.5"	214
30	12	RYAN PULOCK	BRANDON	WHL	RD	6' 0.5"	211
31	8	ROBERT HAGG	MODO JR.	SWEDEN-JR.	LD	6' 2.25"	204
32	36	OLIVER BJORKSTRAND	PORTLAND	WHL	RW	5' 10.75"	166
33	34	JT COMPHER	USA U-18	USHL	LW	5' 10.5"	184
34	47	STEVEN SANTINI	USA U-18	USHL	RD	6' 1.5"	207
35	35	MICHAEL MCCARRON	USA U-18	USHL	RW	6' 5"	228
36	28	LAURENT DAUPHIN	CHICOUTIMI	QMJHL	LC	6' 0"	165
37	7	JACOB DE LA ROSE	LEKSAND	SWEDEN-2	LW	6' 2.25"	190
38	10	PAVEL BUCHNEVICH	CHEREPOVETS 2	RUSSIA-JR.	LW	6' 1"	176
39	11	SHEA THEODORE	SEATTLE	WHL	LD	6' 1.75"	178
40	9	MIRCO MUELLER	EVERETT	WHL	LD	6' 3.25"	184

Rank	CS	PLAYER	Team	League	Pos.	Ht	Wt
41	31	DILLON HEATHERINGTON	SWIFT CURRENT	WHL	LD	6' 3"	196
42	30	JASON DICKINSON	GUELPH	OHL	LC	6' 1.25"	179
43	9	ARTTURI LEHKONEN	KALPA	FINLAND	LW	5' 11"	163
44	44	THOMAS VANNELLI	MINNETONKA	HIGH-MN	RD	6' 2"	165
45	71	REMI ELIE	LONDON	OHL	LW	6' 0.5"	203
46	6	ANDRE BURAKOVSKY	MALMO	SWEDEN-2	LW	6' 1"	178
47	24	IAN MCCOSHEN	WATERLOO	USHL	LD	6' 2.5"	205
48	28	PETER CEHLARIK	LULEA JR.	SWEDEN-JR.	LW	6' 2"	192
49	58	NICK MOUTREY	SAGINAW	OHL	C/LW	6' 2"	208
50	21	JAMES LODGE	SAGINAW	OHL	RC	6' 0.5"	166
51	49	MICHAEL DOWNING	DUBUQUE	USHL	LD	6' 2.75"	192
52	13	LINUS ARNESSON	DJURGARDEN	SWEDEN-2	LD	6' 2"	187
53	NR	PAVEL KOLEDOV	LOKOMOTIV	VHL	RD	6' 0"	181
54	45	CONNOR HURLEY	EDINA HIGH	HIGH-MN	LC	6' 1.25"	174
55	42	ADAM TAMBELLINI	SURREY	BCHL	LC	6' 2.25"	169
56	61	NICHOLAS BAPTISTE	SUDBURY	OHL	RW	6' 0.75"	189
57	3	TRISTAN JARRY	EDMONTON	WHL	G	6'1.25"	183
58	13	ZACH NASTASIUK	OWEN SOUND	OHL	RW	6' 1.25"	190
59	14	VIKTOR CRUS RYDBERG	LINKOPING JR.	SWEDEN-JR.	RC	5' 11"	190
60	63	RYAN KUJAWINSKI	KINGSTON	OHL	LC	6' 1.5"	204
61	40	BRETT PESCE	NEW HAMPSHIRE	H-EAST	RD	6' 2.75"	170
62	56	RYAN FITZGERALD	VALLEY	EJHL	RC	5' 9.5"	170
63	51	GUSTAV OLOFSSON	GREEN BAY	USHL	LD	6' 2.75"	185
64	7	PHILIPPE DESROSIERS	RIMOUSKI	QMJHL	G	6' 1.25"	182
65	48	NICK SORENSEN	QUEBEC	QMJHL	RW	6' 0.75"	174
66	15	WILHELM WESTLUND	FARJESTAD JR.	SWEDEN-JR.	LD	5' 11.25"	184
67	2	ERIC COMRIE	TRI-CITY	WHL	G	6' 0.75"	167
68	12	MARKO DANO	BRATISLAVA	RUSSIA	LC	5' 11"	183
69	26	NIKLAS HANSSON	ROGLE JR.	SWEDEN-JR.	RD	6' 0.5"	175
70	37	JONATHAN DIABY	VICTORIAVILLE	QMJHL	LD	6' 5"	223
71	1	JUUSE SAROS	HPK Hameenlinna	FINLAND	G	5'10"	180
72	100	GREG BETZOLD	PETERBOROUGH	OHL	C/LW	6' 1.5"	195
73	7	SPENCER MARTIN	MISSISSAUGA	OHL	G	6' 2.25"	198
74	38	JUSTIN BAILEY	KITCHENER	OHL	RW	6' 3"	186
75	18	WILLIAM CARRIER	CAPE BRETON	QMJHL	LW	6' 1.5"	198
76	55	JORDAN SUBBAN	BELLEVILLE	OHL	RD	5' 9"	175
77	53	KEATON THOMPSON	USA U-18	USHL	LD	6' 0.25"	187
78	64	TEEMU KIVIHALME	BURNSVILLE	HIGH-MN	LD	5' 11.25"	161
79	23	JUUSO IKONEN	BLUES	FINLAND	LW	5' 9"	169
80	109	BRIAN PINHO	ST. JOHN'S PREP	HIGH-MA	RC	6' 0"	173

Rank	CS	PLAYER	Team	League	Pos.	Ht	Wt
81	11	BOGDAN YAKIMOV	NIZHNEKAMSK 2	RUSSIA-JR.	LC	6' 5"	202
82	29	JOHN HAYDEN	USA U-18	USHL	RC	6' 2.5"	210
83	NR	SVEN ANDRIGHETTO	ROUYN-NORANDA	QMJHL	RW	5'10"	180
84	57	ANTHONY DUCLAIR	QUEBEC	QMJHL	LW	5' 11"	177
85	113	JEFF CORBETT	SUDBURY	OHL	LD	6' 1.5"	170
86	88	CONNOR CLIFTON	USA U-18	USHL	RD	5' 10.75"	175
87	21	RUSHAN RAFIKOV	YAROSLAVL 2	RUSSIA-JR.	LD	6' 2"	181
88	64	GUSTAV POSSLER	MODO JR.	SWEDEN-JR.	RW	6' 0"	183
89	25	ANTON CEDERHOLM	ROGLE JR.	SWEDEN-JR.	LD	6' 1.5"	204
90	51	JOOSE ANTONEN	JYP 2	FINLAND-2	LW/RW	6' 1.5"	183
91	50	YAN PAVEL LAPLANTE	PEI	QMJHL	LC	6' 0"	178
92	70	HUDSON FASCHING	USA U-18	USHL	RW	6' 1.75"	213
93	60	ZACHARY SANFORD	ISLANDERS	EJHL	LW	6' 3"	185
94	73	VINCENT DUNN	VAL-D'OR	QMJHL	LC	5' 11"	172
95	18	CARL DAHLSTROM	LINKOPING JR.	SWEDEN-JR.	LD	6' 3.25"	211
96	89	ATTE MAKINEN	TAPPARA JR.	FINLAND-JR.	RD	6' 3"	206
97	NR	CONNOR CRISP	ERIE	OHL	LC/ LW	6'4"	225
98	166	TYLER GANLY	SOO STE. MARIE	OHL	RD	6' 1"	201
99	135	DANIEL NIKANDROV	SARNIA	OHL	LC	6' 1.5"	191
100	139	DOMINIK KUBALIK	SUDBURY	OHL	LW	6' 1"	181
101	110	KYLE PLATZER	LONDON	OHL	RC	5' 11"	185
102	54	MARC-OLIVIER ROY	BLAINVILLE	QMJHL	LC	6' 0"	175
103	16	LUCAS WALLMARK	SKELLEFTEA JR.	SWEDEN-JR.	LC	5' 10.5"	175
104	145	ERIK BRADFORD	BARRIE	OHL	LC	5' 11.25"	178
105	108	TIM BENDER	MANNHEIM JR.	GERMANY-JR.	LD	6' 0"	174
106	124	NICHOLAS PAUL	BRAMPTON	OHL	LW	6' 2.25"	202
107	150	MILES LIBERATI	LONDON	OHL	LD	5' 11.5"	195
108	79	JEREMY GREGOIRE	BAIE-COMEAU	QMJHL	C/LW	5' 11.75"	190
109	41	ERIC ROY	BRANDON	WHL	LD	6' 2.5"	180
110	43	JAN KOSTALEK	RIMOUSKI	QMJHL	RD	6' 0.5"	181
111	153	GREGORY CHASE	CALGARY	WHL	C/RW	6' 0"	195
112	102	CARTER VERHAEGHE	NIAGARA	OHL	LC	6' 1"	181
113	207	TYLER BERTUZZI	GUELPH	OHL	LW	6' 0"	178
114	85	ROBERTS LIPSBERGS	SEATTLE	WHL	LW	5' 10"	192
115	193	TAYLOR CAMMARATA	WATERLOO	USHL	C/LW	5' 7"	156
116	65	JACKSON HOUCK	VANCOUVER	WHL	RW	6' 0"	186
117	59	MASON GEERTSEN	VANCOUVER	WHL	LD	6' 3"	199
118	104	WILEY SHERMAN	HOTCHKISS	HIGH-CT	LD	6' 5.75"	206
119	101	BEN HARPUR	GUELPH	OHL	LD	6' 5.5"	210
120	72	KURT ETCHEGARY	QUEBEC	QMJHL	LC	5' 11"	185

Rank	CS	PLAYER	Team	League	Pos.	Ht	Wt
121	75	ANTHONY FLORENTINO	SOUTH KENT	HIGH-CT	RD	6' 1"	227
122	17	ANDREI MIRONOV	DYNAMO MOSCOW	RUSSIA	LD	6' 2"	176
123	4	CALVIN PETERSEN	WATERLOO	USHL	G	6' 2.0"	183
124	52	GAB PAQUIN-BOUDREAU	BAIE-COMEAU	QMJHL	LW	5' 11"	167
125	39	NIKOLAI GLUKHOV	OMSK 2	RUSSIA-JR.	RD	6' 2"	178
126	54	DAVID KAMPF	CHOMUTOV JR.	CZREP-JR.	RW	6' 0"	168
127	41	DMITRI YUDIN	ST. PTSBURG 2	RUSSIA-JR.	LD	6' 1"	179
128	128	STEPHEN HARPER	ERIE	OHL	LW	6' 1.25"	200
129	120	COLE CASSELS	OSHAWA	OHL	RC	6' 0"	178
130	90	KAYLE DOETZEL	RED DEER	WHL	RD	6' 2.25"	190
131	80	JAKE GUENTZEL	SIOUX CITY	USHL	LC	5' 9.5"	157
132	118	SERGEY TOLCHINSKY	SOO STE. MARIE	OHL	LW	5' 7.25"	152
133	NR	FELIX GIRARD	BAIE-COMEAU	QMJHL	RC	5'11"	190
134	92	COLE ULLY	KAMLOOPS	WHL	LW	5' 10.75"	164
135	125	BRENT PEDERSEN	KITCHENER	OHL	LW	6' 2"	205
136	123	JOSHUA BURNSIDE	MISSISSAUGA	OHL	LW	5' 11.0"	171
137	87	WILL BUTCHER	USA U-18	USHL	LD	5' 9.5"	191
138	101	TOBIAS LILJENDAHL	DJURGARDEN JR.	SWEDEN-JR.	RC	6' 1.75"	214
139	67	DAVID POPE	WEST KELOWNA	BCHL	LW	6' 2.25"	187
140	172	JERRET SMITH	SEATTLE	WHL	RD	6' 1.5"	198
141	8	PATRIK BARTOSAK	RED DEER	WHL	G	6' 1.0"	187
142	NR	DANNY VANDERWIEL	PLYMOUTH	OHL	LW	6' 0"	210
143	NR	RINAT VALIYEV	INDIANA	USHL	LD	6' 01"	190
144	6	EAMON MCADAM	WATERLOO	USHL	G	6' 2.25"	188
145	74	DYLAN LABBE	SHAWINIGAN	QMJHL	LD	6' 1"	180
146	83	JC LIPON	KAMLOOPS	WHL	RW	5' 11.5"	180
147	66	TYLER LEWINGTON	MEDICINE HAT	WHL	RD	6' 1.0"	189
148	58	ROBIN NORELL	DJURGARDEN JR.	SWEDEN-JR.	LD	5' 11"	189
149	158	ZACH HALL	BARRIE	OHL	LC	5' 10.5"	172
150	24	ALEXANDER HENRIKSSON	FARJESTAD JR.	SWEDEN-JR.	LW	6' 1.75"	190
151	NR	FREDERIK TIFFELS	MUSKEGON	USHL	LW	6' 0	185
152	161	BRODY SILK	SUDBURY	OHL	LC	5' 11.75"	185
153	201	THOMAS ALDWORTH	CUSHING ACADEMY	HIGH-MA	RW	5' 11.5"	179
154	9	ANTOINE BIBEAU	PEI	WHL	G	6' 02.5"	207
155	24	SEAN ROMEO	YOUNGSTOWN	USHL	G	5' 11.75"	166
156	68	LEON BRISTEDT	LINKOPING JR.	SWEDEN-JR.	RW	5' 7.5"	180
157	114	MATTHEW MURPHY	HALIFAX	QMJHL	LD	6' 2"	197
158	136	ALEX KILE	GREEN BAY	USHL	LW	5' 11.25"	190
159	192	TREVOR MOORE	TRI-CITY	USHL	LW	5' 9.25"	170
160	62	SEAN MALONE	USA U-18	USHL	LC	5' 11"	183

Rank	CS	PLAYER	Team	League	Pos.	Ht	Wt
161	78	TY STANTON	MEDICINE HAT	WHL	LD	6' 3.5"	173
162	14	ALEXANDRE BELANGER	ROUYN-NORANDA	QMJHL	G	6' 0.5"	170
163	69	MITCHELL WHEATON	KELOWNA	WHL	LD	6' 4"	228
164	187	TYLER HILL	CHICAGO	USHL	LW	6' 5.75"	220
165	86	LUKE RIPLEY	POWELL RIVER	BCHL	LD	6' 3.75"	181
166	98	CONNOR RANKIN	TRI-CITY	WHL	LW	5' 11.75"	194
167	29	VICTOR OHMAN	MODO JR.	SWEDEN-JR.	LC	5' 8.5"	170
168	164	MACKENZIE WEEGAR	HALIFAX	QMJHL	RD	5' 11.75"	183
169	NR	SHANE KAVANAGH	CUSHING ACADEMY	HIGH-MA	RW	5' 11"	195
170	144	CAMERON BRACE	OWEN SOUND	OHL	C	5' 9.5"	176
171	199	STEPHEN NOSAD	PETERBOROUGH	OHL	RW	5' 11"	188
172	148	GAGE AUSMUS	USA U-18	USHL	LD	6' 0.75"	211
173	156	HUNTER GARLENT	GUELPH	OHL	RC	5' 8.25"	164
174	132	JONNY BRODZINSKI	ST. CLOUD STATE	WCHA	C	6' 0"	202
175	91	MARTIN REWAY	GATINEAU	QMJHL	LW	5' 8"	158
176	77	AVERY PETERSON	GRAND RAPIDS	HIGH-MN	LC	6' 2"	194
177	84	TYLER MOTTE	USA U-18	USHL	LC	5' 9.25"	190
178	157	EVAN ALLEN	USA U-18	USHL	RC	5' 9.75"	201
179	152	JEAN-SEBASTIEN DEA	ROUYN-NORANDA	QMJHL	RC	6' 0"	155
180	185	CONNOR LIGHT	ANDOVER	HIGH-MA	LD	6' 4.75"	198
181	32	VYACHESLAV LESCHENKO	MYTISCHI 2	RUSSIA-JR.	RW	5' 11"	165
182	186	ROSS OLSSON	CEDAR RAPIDS	USHL	RW	6' 4.5"	207
183	12	EVAN COWLEY	WICHITA FALLS	NAHL	G	6' 3.75"	182
184	195	DANIEL LAFONTAINE	AVON OLD FARMS	HIGH-CT	RC	5' 9.5"	160
185	NR	WILL TOFFEY	SALISBURY	HIGH-MA	LD	NA	NA
186	76	SPENSER JENSEN	MEDICINE HAT	WHL	RD	6' 4"	191
187	NR	MACOY ERKAMPS	LETHBRIDGE	WHL	RD	5' 11"	193
188	111	NOLAN DE JONG	VICTORIA	BCHL	LD	6' 2"	173
189	169	RYAN SEGALLA	SALISBURY	HIGH-CT	LD	6' 0.5"	190
190	105	MARC MCNULTY	PRINCE GEORGE	WHL	LD	6' 5.75"	185
191	10	AUSTIN LOTZ	EVERETT	WHL	G	6' 0.0"	188
192	117	MATT BUCKLES	ST. MICHAELS	OJHL	RC	6' 1.25"	205
193	37	FILIP SANDBERG	HV 71 JR.	SWEDEN-JR.	RW	5' 9"	172
194	NR	SAM POVOROZNIOUK	KINGSTON	OHL	LW	5' 10"	183
195	42	TIMOTEJ SILLE	SKALICA JR.	SLOVAKIA-JR.	RW	6' 3"	183
196	138	MILES WOOD	NOBLES	HIGH-MA	LW	6' 0.75"	160
197	NR	JESSE LEES	KELOWNA	WHL	RD	6'0"	180
198	NR	BO PELLAH	ALBERNI VALLEY	BCHL	LD	5'11"	150
199	81	LUCA FAZZINI	LUGANO	SWISS	LW	5' 9"	185
200	96	LUKE JOHNSON	LINCOLN	USHL	C	5' 11"	179

Rank	CS	PLAYER	Team	League	Pos.	Ht	Wt
201	112	KEEGAN KANZIG	VICTORIA	WHL	D	6' 7"	241
202	93	BRENDAN HARMS	FARGO	USHL	RW	5' 11.5"	174
203	171	TOMMY VEILLEUX	VICTORIAVILLE	QMJHL	LW	6' 0"	188
204	20	ANTON SLEPYSHEV	UFA	RUSSIA	LW	6' 2"	194
205	NR	ERIC LOCKE	SAGINAW	OHL	LC	5' 9"	182
206	94	NICK HUTCHISON	AVON OLD FARMS	HIGH-CT	LC	6' 1.75"	178
207	NR	CONNOR BOLAND	PETERBOROUGH	OHL	LD	6' 02"	200
208	81	BLAKE HEINRICH	SIOUX CITY	USHL	D	5' 10.75"	194
209	13	BRENDAN BURKE	PORTLAND	WHL	G	6' 3.0	176
210	122	EETU KOIVISTOINEN	BLUES JR.	FINLAND-JR.	C/LW	6' 2"	201

KEY

HP Rank – HockeyProspect.com Ranking
NHL CS – NHL Central Scouting Ranking

Note: The NHL Central Scouting Rankings were obtained from their final rankings. The number shown is the players ranking within either North American or Europe.

Photo Credits

We want to thank Terry Wilson and Aaron Bell from OHL IMAGES for the use of their OHL, WHL and QMJHL player photos.

We also want to thank all the other photographers who allowed us to show off their work.

hockeyligan.se

WHL, OHL, QMJHL for their photos

The USHL for photos from USHL Images

Elite Prospects

Kyle Scholzen/Seattle Thunderbirds

Alden Reiss

Timothy Kane Photography

Bryan Heim/Portland Winterhawks

Tom Sorenson via USHL, USA Hockey

Slapshots Photography

David Chan

Chris Mast

HockeyProspect.com

Founder

Mark Edwards

Scouts

Mark Edwards
Ryan Yessie
Charles An
Simon Larouche
Sam Roberge
Scott McDougall
Josh Deitell
Kevin Thacker
Dylan Liptrap
Jerome Berube
Robert Blaine
Ron Berman

And a few guys who prefer to remain nameless…

Website and Media

Steve Fitzsimmons, Melissa Perri, Laura Barney , Steven Perko and Michelle Sturino

2013-2014

After the NHL Draft in June we will hard on some new features for next year and attend a few summer scouting events.

Stay up to date with the most recent information leading up to the NHL Draft.

Visit HockeyProspect.com for all your prospect news.

HockeyProspect.com
contact@hockeyprospect.com

1.877.473.7238

OAKVILLE ONTARIO
CANADA

www.ingramcontent.com/pod-product-compliance
Lightning Source LLC
Chambersburg PA
CBHW080556090426
42735CB00016B/3251